MW01169220

A Guide To Contested Divorce In New Jersey

Bari Zell Weinberger, Esq.

FAMILY LAW REFERENCE COLLECTION
Weinberger Law Group

A Guide To Contested Divorce In New Jersey

Table of Contents

About The Author

Bari Z. Weinberger, Esq. is a certified matrimonial law attorney and founding partner of Weinberger Law Group. With offices located throughout New Jersey, Weinberger Law Group is New Jersey's largest law firm dedicated solely to divorce and family law. In addition to working with clients, Ms. Weinberger is the Associate Author of the New Jersey Family Law Practice, 15th Ed., a 5-volume treatise utilized by virtually every family law judge and practitioner in the State of New Jersey.

www.WeinbergerLawGroup.com

Disclaimer

This book provides a general overview of New Jersey divorce and family law matters for informational purposes only. The contents included do not in any way supplement or replace legal advice obtained by a qualified and licensed attorney.

The information provided herein is based solely upon my professional experiences in the areas of New Jersey divorce and family law. While every effort has been made to ensure that the information contained in this book is helpful and of high quality, no representations or warranties of any kind are made with regard to the completeness or accuracy of the included content.

Please note that information provided within this guide is current as of publication date. Due to the complexity and frequency with which the divorce and family laws change, you should consult with a qualified attorney to determine the best course of action for your specific legal needs.

If you require legal advice based on the specifics of your case as it relates to New Jersey laws, please feel free to reach out to our office to schedule a consultation with one of our experienced attorneys. It would be our pleasure to help you.

For more information about other topics related to family law, such as alimony, domestic violence, prenuptial agreements, family mediation, child support and child custody, domestic partnerships, or any other family law related topics, please ask us about our other books. All guides in the series are designed, like this one, to help you to make sound decisions regarding your family's individual situation. Please keep in mind, however, that these books contain general information, and not legal advice. Always direct specific questions about your own situation to an attorney.

Letter from the Author

To resolve a divorce matter in a way that truly feels satisfying and fair, I understand that sometimes it is just not possible to reach a quick and easy divorce settlement out of court. Whether it's about your children's safety, your financial future, or your own well-being, questions and concerns may arise that merit further discussion, and possibly the intervention of the courts, in order to achieve the best terms possible for your divorce.

If you and your spouse are not willing or able to amicably resolve the issues in your case, it is called a "contested" divorce, and your case will be litigated and possibly end up in a trial before a family court judge. I hope that reading this guide helps to familiarize you with the New Jersey family court system and the steps involved in taking your case from its inception to a final trial. In preparing this guide, I have compiled an arsenal of comprehensive information to provide you with tips, illustrations and easy-to-understand explanations of the complex litigation process so that you are better equipped to understand your legal rights.

No matter how far along you may be in your divorce, it is important for you to know that even when your divorce is being litigated you still have choices, including the ongoing option to settle out of court. Many times, a divorce can begin as a contested case, but later becomes an uncontested divorce because the parties found a way to reach agreements and settle their disputes along the way.

As you read this guide, carefully consider the issues in your own divorce, and whether an out-of-court option, such as mediation, could work for you, or if going to trial before a judge is the best option. There is no "right" or "wrong" when it comes to uncontested vs. contested divorce. It is true that in some cases, a judge really is needed to make decisions and having a skilled litigator by your side during that process is essential. In other cases, couples can reach enough common ground to make fair and equitable decisions without the need for litigation, but even still, having a masterful family attorney by your side to negotiate on your behalf is still critical in these situations.

At Weinberger Law Group, our family law attorneys have helped countless clients -- just like you -- to resolve their contested divorce matters. While this guide is comprised of the most up to date information available, please note that it is not intended, nor should it be considered a replacement for legal advice. To best protect your legal interests, it is important to retain the services of an accomplished attorney who exclusively practices in the field of family law.

In formulating the best plan to pursue your New Jersey divorce, one of our family law attorneys would be happy to set up a free consultation. If after reading this guide, you have questions or would like to know more, please do not hesitate to get in contact with us. Remember, decisions that you make today could impact your life for many years to come, so proceed with clarity and certainty.

All my best,
Bari Z. Weinberger

Chapter 1

Contested Divorce in New Jersey

Most people feel tremendous anxiety when first confronting the prospect of divorce. Fear of the unknown is normal. If you know or suspect that your divorce will be contested, that is your divorce will involve a high degree of disagreement and conflict, you have a special need for information. This book outlines procedures that apply to the contested divorce process in New Jersey. While everyone going through a contested divorce will experience it differently, there are aspects that tend to be the same. Understanding these aspects can help make the process a much less stressful one.

What is the Difference Between Contested and Uncontested Divorce?

There are generally two different types of divorce in New Jersey: contested and uncontested. A divorce is contested when spouses are not able to reach a full settlement of all issues prior to trial. When spouses cannot arrive at an agreement, despite perhaps trying divorce mediation or other amicable settlement method, they go to court where a judge will hear their divorce matter and issue a ruling. Typical hot button issues that often trigger contested divorce include such sensitive topics as:

- child custody
- child support
- property division
- debt allocation
- alimony

Consider this example:

Karen and Anthony have been married for 25 years, own a business together, and have three children, two of whom are still minors. After Anthony tells Karen of his plans to divorce her, Karen accuses Anthony of mismanaging their business records and siphoning money to give to his mistress. She believes that more of the business should be given to her in the divorce because of his cheating. On his part, Anthony believes Karen is attempting to alienate him from their children and strongly objects to Karen's unwavering demand for sole custody of their minor children. They tried to meet with a mediator, but remain at loggerheads. After months of wrangling, Anthony and Karen decide it's best to proceed in court and have a judge hear their issues.

What Karen and Anthony are experiencing is a contested divorce. If the pair had been able to come to terms with their issues and reach an agreement before heading to court, their divorce would be considered uncontested.

It is very important to note that many divorces begin as contested cases but later become uncontested cases because the parties are able to settle their disputes earlier than anticipated, thus avoiding court.

Understanding the Contested Divorce Process

No two divorces are alike, and even in a contested case, the number of steps you go through in your divorce will vary depending on how complicated your particular situation is and on how much difference there is between the results you want and the results your spouse wants. Procedures will also vary somewhat depending on the rules of the county in which your case is filed.

> You can find statutes dealing with divorce, dissolution of civil unions, annulment, and divorce from bed and board in *Title 2A, Chapter 34, of the New Jersey Statutes Annotated (N.J.S.A.)*, available on-line from the *official New Jersey Legislature* website, located at: http://bit.ly/njlegislature.

Each county court follows state law and state court rules while also establishing its own rules of procedure. You can obtain more information from an attorney with experience practicing family law in your county.

" Many divorces begin as contested cases, but later become uncontested cases because the parties are able to settle their disputes earlier than anticipated, thus avoiding court. "

Bari Z. Weinberger, Esq.

This book will familiarize you with the court procedures of contested divorce in New Jersey. As you move through your case, you will confront various issues along the way. The most common issues couples going through divorce encounter concern the division of property and debt, the appropriateness or amount and duration of alimony (spousal support), and questions concerning parenting and payment of child support. Even in a very high conflict divorce case, couples are often able to resolve one or more of their major issues. To the extent that you are successful in doing this, you will save time, money, and emotional upheaval. You can find extensive information regarding each of these substantive issues in the other e-books in this series. Take time to focus on each issue separately and learn about the applicable law. This will help you to clarify where the real conflict lies in your case.

> If you believe that you and your spouse may be able to settle your case, or if you want tips about how best to approach the settlement process, see the information on our Weinberger Law Group website on uncontested divorce (http://bit.ly/uncontested).

Chapter 2

Before You Begin: Finding An Attorney

If you have determined that your divorce is not likely to be simple and uncontested, your first step should be to think about finding an attorney. Here's why: while there may be a few people with uncomplicated divorces who can proceed without hiring an attorney, it is never a good idea to try to pursue or defend a contested divorce matter before a judge without some form of attorney assistance.

Before you make any final decisions about who to hire, be sure to carefully weigh your options. The attorney you choose for your divorce can have a profound impact on the progress and eventual outcome of your case. The right attorney can help you maximize positive results while keeping costs down to a manageable level.

In searching for legal representation, look for someone who not only has the needed experience, but also make it a priority to find an attorney who is a good listener to you and who is willing to pay attention to what you really want. Give yourself some time to think about the issues in your case:

- *How contentious do you expect your case to be?*
- *Is the conflict primarily because your spouse is blocking every request you have, or are you the one who is unhappy with demands your spouse is making?*
- *What are the major points of disagreement?*
- *Are there any issues that you and your spouse agree on or are likely to reach agreement on fairly easily?*

These are all questions you will want to discuss in a consultation with any attorney with whom you are considering working.

As you make contact with various law firms, also be prepared to ask an attorney what all possible outcomes might be in your case. If an attorney tries to discourage you from following a particular course of action, make sure that you understand the reasons for this recommendation. It is not unusual for people embarking on the divorce process to start out with one plan and end up with another.

You may have to make some difficult decisions along the way. The attorney you ultimately choose should have the ability to help you make the best choices possible under all of the circumstances of your unique case.

Scheduling a Consultation

Once you have a good idea of the basic qualifications you are seeking, schedule consultations with two or three different attorneys who meet these criteria. This will help you get a good sense of some of the more subtle ways that two similar attorneys can differ from one another in personal philosophy and style. Most attorneys charge a fee for an initial consultation; some will offer a complimentary appointment of thirty minutes to an hour. If you decide to take advantage of one or more of these complimentary appointments, be cautious. You can obtain very useful information this way, but make sure that you are comfortable before making a final decision and signing a retainer agreement.

When consulting with an attorney, it pays to be efficient and make the maximum use of your time. Prepare a detailed list of questions and concerns before your meeting and be sure to write down the answers you get. Ask follow-up questions if you do not understand something. Attorneys are used to using fairly technical language, but a good attorney will be able to break everything down into terms that a client can easily understand.

Later in this chapter you will find a list of specific questions that you may want to ask any attorney you are thinking about hiring. Review this list and consider how each question may apply to your personal situation. Add your own questions to the list.

Attorney Qualifications

These are some of the things you may want to consider when narrowing down your list of candidates:

1. Family Law Experience

While a good rapport is certainly an important consideration in choosing an attorney, the attorney's experience and skill is even more important. Many people embarking on the divorce process will have a friend, or a friend of a friend, who practices law. Before automatically assuming that this person would be a good choice, be sure to take into account that the practice of law today is highly specialized. A personal recommendation is certainly reassuring, but be careful about hiring any attorney who does not have significant experience in family law. Someone whose practice includes a large proportion of family law matters will almost always be a better choice than someone who handles such cases on only an occasional basis. This is particularly critical if you anticipate a high degree of conflict in your case. An attorney who practices New Jersey family law exclusively and is intimately familiar with the state's laws, court system, and recent court decisions, will be well-equipped to handle your case. When interviewing a prospective attorney, ask specific questions about family law experience. Do not accept vague answers or explanations, and be especially cautious about trusting advertisements.

2. Certifications

One way to be sure that your attorney has substantial experience in family law is to choose someone who has been state-certified in the specialty. While not all states have a certification process for attorneys practicing family law, New Jersey does. The designation "*Certified by the Supreme Court as a Matrimonial Law Attorney*" is an official honor received by only about 2% of all New Jersey attorneys. Only attorneys who have demonstrated superior knowledge and experience across a broad range of issues arising in family law practice are entitled to use this designation.

To be certified in matrimonial law in New Jersey, an attorney must demonstrate at least the following:

- a minimum of five years in good standing as a member of the New Jersey bar,
- ongoing completion of continuing legal education requirements specifically tailored to family law,
- very specific and substantial experience in matrimonial law,
- favorable evaluations from other attorneys and judges, and
- an acceptable grade on a written examination covering principles of matrimonial law.

3. Firm Size

The size of the firm you hire may have some important implications for how your case is handled. Some people feel that a sole practitioner will offer more personalized attention. This may or may not be true, depending on the individual lawyer and the overall circumstances. Many sole practitioners handle multiple cases at once and find themselves with limited time when several different matters need attention at the same time. They often rely heavily on support staff (to the extent that they have support staff) and sometimes work with another sole practitioner or an independent contract attorney to lighten the load when things get too busy.

On the other hand, some attorneys in larger firms delegate much of their work to associate attorneys or paralegals. The number of cases an attorney handles at once and how often an attorney communicates directly with a client may be more related to personal style than to firm size. Delegation is not necessarily a negative, as it can help to keep costs down, but it is important to know what to expect and who will be working on your file.

When you interview a potential attorney, find out as much as you can about the attorney's support staff, current caseload, and division of responsibilities in the office. Ask who you will be communicating with on a regular basis and who will handle your case if an emergency comes up and your primary attorney is in court, on vacation, or otherwise not available.

4. Approach to Litigation

Family law attorneys who have their clients' best interests at heart are generally settlement oriented and will look for ways to amicably work things out. They deal respectfully with opposing counsel and will urge you to be cooperative in openly and promptly providing information to the other side. They will often suggest mediation as an appropriate option. If you are anticipating a conflict-ridden case, you may be harboring a lot of negative emotion toward your spouse, making a cooperative approach feel counterintuitive. Unfortunately, there are some lawyers who will be all too eager to support negative emotions, leading clients to feel justified in escalating battle. While this may provide temporary validation, in the long run, it is almost always damaging.

" The right attorney can help you maximize positive results, while keeping costs down to a manageable level. "

Bari Z. Weinberger, Esq.

5. Avoid Overly Aggressive Attorneys

Forcing the other side to file papers and make multiple court appearances can lead to motion after motion being argued in court—which means costs will soon spiral rapidly out of control. Ask the attorney what the likelihood is of your case settling prior to trial. Trials are extremely expensive. A lawyer who goes to trial frequently in family law matters may be overly aggressive. Even if you know you will have to fight for what you need in your divorce, you will almost always be better served by an attorney who is a skilled negotiator first and a gladiator in the courtroom only when necessary.

On the other hand, of course, if you anticipate a heavily contested divorce, you will need an attorney whose negotiating skills are backed up by powerful abilities in the courtroom. Carefully assess an attorney's litigation experience. Consider whether or not the attorney has enough confidence not to back down in a critical situation and enough experience to know when going to court is the best available option. Some family law attorneys have no trial experience, and some restrict their practice to collaborative law and never go to court. These are not going to be good choices if you know that there is a high probability that your case will end up in the courtroom.

6. Cost & Retainer Fees

The overall cost of any legal matter can be difficult to predict at the outset of a case. While an attorney's hourly fee is one consideration, a highly skilled attorney with many years of experience may be able to accomplish certain tasks in a fraction of the time a less experienced attorney would need.

This is why retainer fees can sometimes be deceiving. Attorneys require a new client to enter into an agreement outlining rights and responsibilities and provide a retainer as an advance payment against work to be performed. A common misconception is that a law firm that requires a smaller retainer will charge less overall for the entire matter. In reality, the amount of the initial retainer is not based on how much work or how many hours will ultimately be necessary to resolve a case. Some law firms charge a lower retainer to lure potential clients into signing up for their services. Try to get as much of an idea as possible up front regarding the potential costs of each aspect of your case.

7. Specialized Knowledge and Experience

If you have a case that may be especially complicated in a particular area, it is a good idea to ask about the lawyer's expertise in that specific area. For example, if you own a business, find out if the attorney has experience in working with divorcing clients with similar types of business. Some family law attorneys have carved out a niche or sub-specialty within the broader practice area. An attorney who is highly skilled in complex financial distributions, for example, may have little or no expertise in child custody matters.

8. Personal Philosophy

In some cases it may help to have an idea of the attorney's personal philosophy about certain matters. For example, if you are a parent who feels strongly about a particular type of child custody arrangement, you would probably not want to hire an attorney who has a strong opposing point of view. Be clear about what results you are looking for at the very first meeting. If the attorney discourages you from pursuing any particular course of action, find out why. It may be for a valid legal reason, but it could also be rooted in personal bias.

9. Analysis of your Case

Make sure the attorney outlines the drawbacks of your situation as well as the upside. Lawyers sometimes create unrealistic expectations in the hopes of being hired by a client, and a good lawyer will clarify the negative aspects of your case as well as the positive ones. While it may not be pleasant to look reality so squarely in the face, an overly optimistic view of your case could set you up for an ugly surprise down the road. It is important to understand that lawyers can only work within a given set of facts and the applicable law; even the most skillful attorney can never promise a certain result, and results in family law are notoriously unpredictable.

Questions to Ask an Attorney during an Initial Consultation

The following questions address various aspects of legal representation that you may want to assess in your initial consultation with an attorney:

Skills and Experience:

- How long have you been practicing family law?
- What percentage of your practice is family law?
- Are you certified in matrimonial law or is the head of the firm certified?
- Do you have any other specialized education or training in family law?
- If so, what is the specific nature of the education or training?
- How many family law trials have you handled?
- How many other family law court procedures have you handled?

Basic Strategy:

- Do you generally recommend mediation?
- Do you recommend collaborative law?
- What percentage of your caseload goes to trial?
- How many of your cases settle through mediation?
- Under what circumstances might you feel that filing a motion in court or taking a case through the trial stage is the best option?

Specialized Knowledge:

- Do you have more experience in one area of family law (e.g., child custody, child support, property distribution, alimony) than in others?
- Are you personally familiar with experts (e.g., accountants, child psychologists, appraisers, private investigators) that may be relevant in any particular aspect of my case?

Case Management:

- How many attorneys are in your firm?
- Will you personally handle my case?
- Who will provide back-up if you are unavailable?
- Who will I be communicating with on a regular basis?
- How often do you accept or return phone calls?
- Do you prefer to communicate primarily by phone or primarily by email?

Costs:

- Will you require a retainer before starting work on my case?
- How much is the retainer?
- What is your hourly fee?
- What is the hourly fee of others in your firm who may be working on my case?
- What fees might I expect to incur as a result of hiring other professionals (e.g., accountants, child psychologists, appraisers, private investigators)?

- What other costs will I be responsible for beyond hourly fees?
- What are some of the different scenarios and contingencies that may affect the ultimate cost of my divorce?

Practical Tip: Break down individual costs for a better understanding of overall costs.

The retainer: The "retainer" is simply a down payment against which your lawyer will bill costs. When the retainer is used up, if additional work is required, you will have to pay more. Whether you pay a large retainer or a small one, the important thing is to get an estimate of how much each phase of your case will actually cost.

The hourly attorney fee: Family attorneys bill by the hour, in fractional increments. Be sure that you understand how this will work. Often attorneys bill in tenths of an hour, or 6 minute increments, which you may see on your bill as .1 hours (6 minutes), .5 hours (30 minutes), etc. Some attorneys may bill in a different increment, such as a quarter of an hour. This could result in a substantial cost disparity over time. For example, if an attorney charges $300 per hour and bills in tenths of an hour, five phone calls of six minute each would be $150. If an attorney charges $300 per hour and bills in quarter hours, the same five phone calls of six minutes each would be $375.

Court fees, copy fees, postage, and more: Read your fee agreement carefully. In addition to your attorney's hourly fee, in most cases, you will have to pay for copying costs, court filing costs, telephone and fax charges, delivery fees, and other miscellaneous costs. Legal cases are very paper-intensive. Copy fees alone can quickly add up. Ask the attorney what the typical filing fees and delivery fees are likely to be for each phase of your case.

Expert fees: Few people embarking on a divorce comprehend how quickly expert fees can accumulate in a case. If you are considering using experts, find out what this might cost at the very outset of your case. Your whole strategy could change when you have accurate information.

- - - - -

FAQ: What If I Cannot Afford An Attorney?

If you find an attorney you would like to work with but you do not believe that you can afford the representation, discuss creative possibilities for financing your case with the attorney. You may be surprised to find that you can work out the payments with less difficulty than you first thought. Remember that a good attorney often saves you money in the long run. On the other hand, if you have very low income and few assets, you may find that you truly are unable to afford the services of any of the attorneys you would like to hire. If you find yourself in this position, contact Legal Services of New Jersey at their official website, found at: http://bit.ly/lsnj, to determine whether or not you are eligible for low cost assistance.

- - - - -

Chapter 3

Preparing to Meet with an Attorney

Before you have an initial consultation or first appointment with an attorney, gather together as much information about your financial situation as possible and begin to assemble supporting documents. Collecting documents can be a daunting task and it is not necessary to have everything pulled together prior to the first meeting. Still, the more details you can provide at an initial consultation, the more useful and specific the advice will be from the lawyer regarding options and potential outcomes in your case.

If you are not able to gather complete records, try at least to obtain up-to-date information about your financial circumstances. For example, how many financial accounts you and your spouse have, what type of accounts they are and whether they are in joint names or individually titled. Be prepared with account numbers and current balances. Find out what property you own either separately or together, when and how it was acquired, and its approximate equity and market value. Obtain current information about the nature and probable value of any business either of you own. Know who your insurance carriers are for policies covering health, life, homeowners, and auto, and if applicable, who the beneficiaries are. Be sure to evaluate your debt as well as your assets. Know what the debt is for, when and by whom it was acquired, and how it is currently being paid. If you and your spouse are living apart, provide an estimate of each household's expenses and indicate how these are currently covered, particularly if one of you is providing financial assistance to the other, or paying expenses for children living in a different household.

The most important documents to bring to an initial meeting are those that verify the current income of both you and your spouse, such as tax returns, recent pay stubs, and W-2 forms, as well as copies of any court documents already filed in your case, any papers you have been served with that may require a response, and any premarital or marital agreements between you and your spouse.

You may eventually need to produce documents showing all or most of the following:

Income and Investments for the Past One to Three Years (unless otherwise noted)

- W-2 statements for the past three to five years for you and your spouse,
- the three most recent pay stubs from your employer,
- state and federal individual and business income tax returns,
- monthly bank statements for all joint and individual accounts,
- monthly statements for all stocks, bonds and mutual funds any trust documents affecting you, your spouse, or your children,
- documents showing income on any investment properties, such as rent receipts,
- account statements for annuities, certificates of deposit, 529 accounts, UTMA/UGMA accounts, or other financial accounts in the name of you, your spouse, or any of your children,
- current social security statements for you and your spouse, and
- statements for all retirement accounts, including pensions, 401(k)s and 403(b)s, IRAs, SERPs, SEPs, ESOPs, or any other retirement-type accounts.

Property Ownership

- deeds and purchase documents for your primary residence,
- deeds and purchase documents for any other real property holdings, including rental properties or vacation homes,

- ownership documents for any business property owned partially or fully by either you or your spouse, with evidence of percentage ownership,
- purchase documents or appraisals for any personal property of significant value (antiques, collectables, jewelry, art, furs, etc.),
- registration certificates or title documents for automobiles or other vehicles, and
- documents evidencing separate ownership of property by either spouse, including a list of property owned prior to marriage, a list of any purchases made with such property, and any documents evidencing an inheritance by either spouse.

Bills and Outstanding Debt for the Past One to Three Years

- property tax statements,
- mortgage statements,
- credit card statements, whether joint or individual,
- vehicle or equipment leases,
- tax liens or notices from the IRS,
- utility bills,
- student loan documents or tuition bills,
- any other loans or notes payable,
- outstanding medical bills,
- arrearages on prior spousal or child support orders or agreements, and
- a monthly budget worksheet (QuickBooks, Quicken, Case Information Statement).

" The more details you can provide about your financial situation at your consultation, the more specific the advice from your attorney can be regarding your options in your case. "

Bari Z. Weinberger, Esq.

Legal Documents

- any documents already filed in court,
- any court papers you have been served with,
- any prenuptial or marital agreements,
- wills,
- living wills,
- powers of attorney,
- advance healthcare directives or healthcare proxies,
- pre-nuptial or post-nuptial agreements,
- divorce judgments, marital separation agreements, or support orders from any previous marriage,
- any other lawsuits, judgments, or garnishments, and
- business partnership agreements and financial records.

Insurance Documents

- health insurance documents indicating carrier, policy and group numbers, and persons covered,
- life insurance declaration page indicating carrier, policy number, face amount, cash value, insured, and beneficiaries,
- auto insurance declaration page indicating carrier, policy number, vehicles covered, insured, and term,
- homeowner's insurance declaration page indicating carrier, policy number, and residence covered,

- long-term care insurance declaration page indicating carrier, policy number, and insured, and
- disability insurance documents indicating carrier, policy number, and insured.

Additional Information

When you are ready to file or respond to a complaint for divorce, your attorney also will need to know the following:

- the date and place of your marriage,
- whether both you and your spouse have made a definite decision to divorce,
- the reasons for the divorce,
- the names, ages, social security numbers, and current addresses for yourself, your spouse and any children you have, including any step-children or children from previous relationships who live with either you or your spouse or are the subject of any child support agreements or orders affecting either you or your spouse,
- any health issues affecting you, your spouse or a child,
- all previous marriages for either of you,
- any current child custody and support arrangements, and
- any known or anticipated problems relating to children.

Review Your Goals:

After providing the initial information, be sure to let your attorney know what results you would like to see in your case. Clarify exactly where the areas of conflict are and how extreme the conflict is likely to be. Consider any of the following areas applicable to your situation:

- **Child custody**: Which parent will serve as the primary residential parent? Are you and your spouse likely to agree about this?

- **Visitation plan**: Start thinking about possible options that might work for the whole family. Fill out a blank calendar with your initial scheduling ideas.

- **Marital home**: Who is currently living in the home? Will you or your spouse remain there, and if so, for how long? Will you sell the home, or will one of you buy out the other's interest?

- **Other assets and debt division**: What resolution do you consider reasonable? Are there any assets such as businesses that need to stay with one spouse or the other for practical reasons? If the division of assets will be unbalanced, is this fair? If not, can the balance be equalized in some way?

- **Spousal support / alimony**: Is this likely to be a factor? Does one of you have a much higher income than the other? Has one spouse been financially dependent for an extended period of time?

- **Attorney's fees and expenses**: What will be the source of payment? Are there joint accounts that are able to cover legal fees?

- **Beneficiaries of insurance policies**: Health insurance may be tied to one spouse's employment. Will this change? Will either spouse want to change beneficiaries on life insurance or other policies?

Chapter 4

Working with Your Lawyer: What to Expect

Think of your working relationship with your lawyer as a business partnership. You deserve to have a clear understanding of what to expect. Your retainer agreement will detail the terms of your understanding. This is a binding contract; you should read the entire agreement and request clarification of anything you do not understand before signing it.

There are certain things your lawyer needs from you to be able to provide you with the highest quality of legal representation. A cooperative attitude, realistic goals, and a clear head will steer you in the right direction. If your attorney requests information from you, provide it as quickly as possible, and make sure that it is accurate and complete. Keep written explanations clear, concise, and factual. Regardless of how tempted you may be to keep certain information to yourself, never hide anything from your attorney.

Your lawyer should discuss the likelihood of desirable results, as well as all other possible outcomes; and then work with you to come up with a strategy for your case, including planning for different contingencies depending on uncertain variables. If you are having trouble developing a strategy that both you and the lawyer feel is workable, take a hard look at any possible reasons for this. Are you expecting too much? Are you committed to pursuing a course of action that is expensive and has a low probability of success? Understand that your lawyer cannot perform miracles and can only accomplish results within the confines of the law and the court system. If you insist on pursuing a course of action after your attorney has advised you that it has a low probability of success, and you fail to get the results you hoped for, you will still have to pay your attorney.

Explore your finances early in the case and be sure you understand what sources you have available to pay for your legal fees. Your attorney can help you with ideas for financing if money is tight. If you have to liquidate assets with your spouse or request temporary orders for support or attorney's fees from the court, these matters should be handled as early as possible. Make sure you understand your legal invoices, and do not be afraid to ask questions.

Pay bills promptly so that your attorney can concentrate on what needs to be done in your case.

Preparation will go a long way toward controlling costs. Prepare in advance for telephone calls with your attorney. Have your questions organized so that you can ask them all in the same call. Try to refrain from using your lawyer as a therapist. While many family law attorneys are wonderful to talk to, a lawyer is not usually trained as a therapist and often charges more per hour than a therapist would.

Divorce is very stressful and many clients have difficulty handling powerful emotions during their legal case. This is natural and expected. The good news is that it does not go on forever. In the meantime, do not hesitate to consult a therapist if you need help gaining control over difficult emotions.

Practical Tip: Consider The Need For Other Professionals In Your Case.

While your attorney will be the most important professional involved in your case and the person you need to work with first, there are several other professionals who may participate to various degrees as your case develops. Your attorney can explain the purpose and roles of such professionals, and in some cases, can help you select them. You can also find more information about these other professionals throughout this handbook. Keep a list of names and phone numbers of any experts you or your spouse hire or the court appoints in your case.

" A co-operative attitude, realistic goals and a clear head are essential…and never hide anything from your attorney. "

Bari Z. Weinberger, Esq.

Other Professionals

You may find yourself relying on one or more of the following professionals:

Accountant – If you do not already have a personal accountant or tax adviser, you may find the need for one now. An accountant can help you organize your financial records and provide tax advice throughout your case. Accountants also may act as experts in cases requiring professional opinions about valuation of assets, such as family businesses. These accountants often have additional specialized training.

Actuary – If valuation of an asset involves significant elements of future uncertainty and risk, you may need an actuary. This is particularly likely to be true in a pension valuation.

Appraiser – Appraisers are qualified to give estimates on the value of a home or other property.

Certified Divorce Planner – A divorce planner can explain how different financial scenarios may play out over time. This can be very valuable if you are considering trading one asset for another or others (retirement funds for a home, for example) in a settlement. Divorce planners are often accountants.

Child Custody Expert – If you and your spouse have a parenting dispute you cannot resolve, you may need a forensic psychologist, best interest custody expert or parent coordinator.

Computer Forensic Expert –These experts specialize in electronic data, such as text messages, emails and computer search histories. They can use software tools to perform functions such as reconstructing deleted files. A computer forensic expert may also be a licensed private investigator (in some states this is required).

Counselor or Therapist – A counselor or therapist can be a major source of emotional support for you or for your children during this difficult process.

Employability or Vocational Expert – This kind of expert can be used to resolve issues regarding the employability or earning capacity of an unemployed or underemployed spouse. The expert can present testimony regarding available jobs and salaries that fit the spouse's education and experience.

Guardian *ad litem* – In some child custody disputes a court will appoint a separate attorney for the children. This person is called a law guardian, or guardian "*ad litem*."

Mediator – A divorce mediator is a neutral third party who works to help a couple achieve a mutually acceptable settlement. Ideally, a mediator will also be a family law attorney or retired family law judge who will be familiar with the specifics of family law.

Medical, Mental Health or Social Experts – These professionals can offer opinions in an alimony or child support analysis regarding the employability of a spouse claiming to be disabled, or can evaluate the potential impact of a health condition on one spouse's parenting abilities. If there are issues regarding child abuse, and the

Division of Child Protection and Permanency (DCP&P) is involved in your case, a social worker will generally be assigned to investigate the charges.

Private Investigator – Private investigators can help you gather detailed information about your spouse's financial situation or behavior.

Chapter 5

Initiating the Divorce Process

The process of contested divorce is filled with contingencies. People embarking on the process usually want to know how much time it will take. Unfortunately, this is impossible to predict in advance. Judges and attorneys in New Jersey strive to comply with court guidelines known as "best practices," which recommend resolution of all cases within one year of the filing of a complaint.

Initiating the Divorce Process

Resolution of all cases within one year of filing is not always possible. Factors such as the number of contested issues, the other spouse's level of cooperation, the necessity of hiring experts, and whether or not such experts produce reports in a timely fashion, can all have a substantial impact on the progress of a case.

The courts have implemented many procedures designed to speed up the process and facilitate efforts to resolve contested matters. The following is a general outline of the steps in a contested New Jersey divorce. Not all cases will go through every phase of the process, and parties are always free to settle a case at any stage.

> *If you would like to see a graphic outline of these steps, you can follow along with Weinberger Law Group's Divorce Road Map, located at: http://bit.ly/divorce-roadmap.*

In a contested divorce, you will normally have an attorney prepare all of your paperwork. Even so, it is important that you stay very closely involved and that you understand how the process works. The following information will help you become familiar with the procedures involved as you move through the New Jersey divorce process.

Preparing a Complaint

All married couples begin an action for divorce in New Jersey with a Complaint for Divorce*. The person who files the complaint is the "plaintiff" and the other party is the "defendant."

If you are ending a domestic partnership or a civil union, the procedural steps you will follow are virtually the same as those you would follow in pursuing a divorce. Domestic partnership terminations tend to involve fewer legal issues than either divorces or dissolutions of civil unions, but the procedures are still essentially the same. If you entered into a legal marriage, civil union, or domestic partnership in another state or country and then moved to New Jersey, you will be able to formally terminate your relationship in New Jersey once you have satisfied the residency requirements.

Residency Requirements

For a New Jersey court to have jurisdiction over a divorce, at least one of the spouses must be a resident of the county in which the case is filed, and in most cases, one spouse must have been a resident of the state for the entire one-year period immediately preceding initiation of the case.

In divorce actions based on adultery, there is no specific time requirement.

Special Residency Requirements for Servicemembers

In general, a servicemember or spouse of a servicemember may choose to file a complaint for divorce in the state where the spouse resides, in the state where the servicemember is stationed, or in the state where the servicemember claims legal residence. The latter can be either the servicemember's home state or the state where the servicemember plans to live after leaving the service. The home state or "home of record" will be designated in the servicemember's periodic payment record, known as the Leave and Earnings Statement (LES).

If you are in the service or married to someone in the service you should think carefully about when and where to initiate a divorce case. While filing a complaint where the servicemember is currently stationed may be convenient in the short-term, it will be much less convenient if that state retains jurisdiction after both of you have moved to different states. A court will normally grant a motion to transfer jurisdiction if neither party remains in the state, but if spouses or former spouses reside in different states and each wants the matter transferred to a different court, the motion could be conflict-ridden, time-consuming, and expensive.

If the two of you have children together, you will also need to consider the children's residency. Pursuant to the Uniform Child Custody Jurisdiction and Enforcement Act (UCCJEA), a state court will not ordinarily have jurisdiction over matters of child custody unless the children have physically resided in that state for at least the past six months. So, for example, if you have been living in Virginia with your children for the past six months and you decide to file for divorce in New Jersey where your military spouse is stationed, the New Jersey family court would not be able to enter orders controlling the custody and visitation of your children.

" The Complaint for Divorce must state the reason for divorce, known as 'grounds.'

Bari Z. Weinberger, Esq.

Information to Include in the Complaint

If you are the plaintiff, you will generally have to provide the following information:

- name and current address for both you and your spouse*,
- the date and place of your marriage,
- the grounds for divorce, and any necessary supporting information (such as timing of breakdown of marriage, date of separation or description of alleged cruel acts),
- confirmation that the residency requirement has been satisfied,
- any additional addresses you used during the time the grounds for divorce arose,
- names and ages of any children,
- list of any prior legal actions between you and your spouse, and
- description of the relief you are requesting in the case.

Victims of domestic violence have the option of providing a post office box number or substitute address and phone number.

Grounds

The complaint must state a reason for the divorce, known as "grounds." While many people are used to thinking of the plaintiff in a lawsuit as someone who is making an accusation of wrongdoing against a defendant, this is not usually the case in a divorce. Although some plaintiffs do choose a fault-based ground, there is rarely any advantage to doing so. People also sometimes combine different fault-based grounds, such as adultery and extreme cruelty, but this is generally unnecessary. The choice of grounds will have little or no bearing on eventual court decisions regarding matters such as alimony, child custody and support, or property division. Nevertheless, if you believe that you have one or more fault grounds for divorce, consult a knowledgeable New Jersey family law attorney before deciding which grounds to choose for your complaint.

Fault-based grounds available in New Jersey include:

- **Extreme Cruelty.** The behavior required to satisfy the ground of extreme cruelty is not necessarily "extreme." Any behavior that would lead a reasonable person to conclude that the spouse initiating the divorce is justified in not wanting to continue the marriage will satisfy the requirement; however, a plaintiff must include details of the alleged behavior in the complaint. As most defendants understandably react negatively to an accusation of cruelty, whether extreme or not, choosing this ground may set off a contentious process.

- **Adultery**. A spouse may file for divorce on the ground of adultery even if neither spouse has resided in New Jersey for a full year; however, for a court to grant a divorce on this basis, the plaintiff must disclose and prove all of the relevant facts. In addition, the other person alleged to have had the affair (called the "co-respondent") must also be served. The process of complying with this requirement often increases hostility between divorcing spouses. If you are the plaintiff and you are considering starting a divorce case with a claim of adultery, be sure to consider the ramifications and consult an attorney regarding the legal benefit of making such a claim.

- **Desertion**. Divorce based on desertion requires proof that one spouse has "abandoned" the other for a minimum of 12 months. The abandonment the law requires is not a physical leaving of the home, but rather a lack of physical intimacy between the spouses for the required period of time.

- **Other Fault Grounds**. A few additional fault-based grounds still exist in New Jersey, but they are rarely used as most people find them to be inconvenient or inapplicable for various reasons. Such grounds include habitual drunkenness, narcotic addiction, incarceration, institutionalization due to mental illness, and deviant sexual acts.

The great majority of spouses filing for divorce in New Jersey choose a "no-fault" ground. It is important to understand that choosing a no-fault ground does not mean that you will be unable to contest issues in your divorce. Even if you are not in agreement regarding some major aspect of your divorce such as property division, alimony, or child custody, choosing a no-fault ground avoids provoking a defensive reaction on the part of the spouse receiving the complaint, and thus helps to avoid escalating conflict right from the outset.

Grounds available for divorce without any allegation of fault include:

- **Irreconcilable Differences.** This refers to a breakdown of the marriage lasting 6 months or longer, without a reasonable prospect of reconciliation. The parties are not required to provide any information about the circumstances leading to the breakdown.

- **Separation**. Couples who have lived apart for at least 18 months can file for divorce on the basis of separation. No other circumstances are necessary.

The New Jersey law describing grounds for divorce is N.J.S.A 2A:34-2. For more information on grounds for divorce in New Jersey, see the Weinberger Law Group website at: http://bit.ly/divorcegrounds.

Request for Relief:

Although the specifics of whatever relief you are requesting, such as dollar amounts for support or detailed schedules for parenting time, can be left to work out later, it is important to include in your complaint a general request for any relief you believe you may need at any point during the development of your case. If you already have a signed Marital Settlement Agreement ("MSA"), you can indicate the relief you and your spouse have included in the MSA.

A New Jersey divorce complaint can include a request for some or all of the following relief (and more):

- alimony (also known as spousal support or spousal maintenance),
- equitable property distribution, including division of real and personal property and allocation of debts,
- custody of minor children,
- parenting time with minor children,
- child support, and
- restoration of former name.

Filing Documents with the Court

New Jersey Court Rules require a plaintiff in a divorce case to file the complaint in the county where the cause of action (grounds for divorce) arose. This may be the county where either spouse currently resides, or, depending on the facts included in the complaint, may be a county of previous residence. If you are uncertain where to file your case, an attorney can advise you. After determining where to file, you, or your attorney, should send the court the original and two copies of your complaint and all supporting documents, and keep two additional copies of everything filed for your own records. For an article presenting a good overview of the documents required in a New Jersey divorce case, see "New Jersey Divorce Documents: Prominent New Jersey Family Law Attorney Explains the Rules," by Bari Z. Weinberger, Esq. on the Weinberger Law Group website: http://bit.ly/divorce-documents.

Depending on the circumstances of your particular case, you will need to file all or most of the following with your complaint:

- **Certification of Verification and Non-Collusion**. This is a sworn statement attached to the complaint verifying that all of the claims and facts included are true; that there are no other actions currently pending in a court or arbitration venue involving you and your spouse (or identifying any actions that are pending); and that there are no other people who should be named in the current case.

- **Certification of Insurance**. This is a form attached to the complaint listing all known insurance coverage for you, your spouse, and your minor children, including health, life, homeowners or renters, automobile, or any other type of insurance. Coverage in effect at the date of filing cannot be cancelled during the case without court approval or consent of the parties.

- **Certification of Notification of Complementary Dispute Resolution Alternatives**. This is a form attached to the complaint which states that you have received information from the court or your attorney explaining the availability of dispute resolution alternatives such as mediation and arbitration. If you are represented by an attorney, the attorney must provide you with this information and will also sign the certification.

- **Family Part Case Information Statement (CIS)**. A CIS is a financial disclosure statement requiring detailed financial information and copies of certain documents such as tax returns and pay stubs. Both spouses are required to file a CIS within 20 days of a defendant's answer or appearance in any New Jersey case in which there are contested issues regarding children, property division, or spousal support. Even if you have settled all of your issues, it is always a good idea for both spouses to file a CIS, as this helps ensure full disclosure of all financial information on both sides and will bolster the enforceability of any MSA the spouses enter into. You must update your CIS any time there is a change in financial circumstances, and you must keep a copy of it until the conclusion of all financial matters in your case, including completion of any required alimony payments.

- **Confidential Litigant Information Sheet (CLIS)**. You must include this form if you are requesting alimony or child support. It contains detailed personal information, including date and place of birth, social security number, driver's license number, license plate number, mother's maiden name, children's social security numbers, and medical information. It is not attached to the complaint and is kept out of the public record as a confidential document. The purpose of the form is to provide information that will enable the court to contact you when necessary to establish, modify, or enforce orders in your case.

- **Request for Waiver of Fees and Supporting Certification and Order Waiving Fees**. If you are unable to afford the court filing fees you may be eligible for a fee waiver. You must submit the appropriate forms with a waiver request.

- **Filing Fees and Self-Addressed Stamped Envelope**. To complete the filing and return date-stamped copies of the filed documents, the court will require a cover letter requesting such copies, payment of any applicable filing fees, and a self-addressed, stamped envelope large enough to hold the copies being returned. If you are represented by an attorney, your attorney will take care of all of these details for you.

Serving the Complaint

After you file your complaint, you must serve it on your spouse, following the exact procedures required by court rules. If you are represented by an attorney, the attorney will let you know the best method for your particular situation. Generally, service can be by any of the following methods:

- **Service by Mail**. This is usually the cheapest and easiest method of service. If you know that your spouse will accept service, you can serve your papers by regular and certified mail, return receipt requested. Your spouse will have to sign and notarize an acknowledgment of service and return it to you. You will then file the acknowledgment with the court. If your spouse is represented by an attorney, the attorney can generally also accept service on your spouse's behalf.

- **Personal Service**. If you do not believe that your spouse will accept service voluntarily, you can have the sheriff's office or a process server personally serve your papers. There will be a fee for this service which will vary depending on mileage and number of trips required to effect service. You may be able to have the service fees waived if you have qualified for a waiver of filing fees and your spouse resides within New Jersey. If your spouse is living out of state, the procedure will generally be the same although the fees may be slightly higher. If your spouse is living in a foreign country the process may be more complicated and you should consult an attorney to ensure correct service.

- **Substituted Service on a Special Agent or Service by Publication**. These methods are available if you do not know your spouse's whereabouts and cannot determine them after diligent inquiry. These methods are more complicated and may require the assistance of an attorney.

Responding to a Complaint

A defendant has 35 days from the date of service to respond to the complaint. The parties can agree to an extension of up to 60 days by signing a stipulation before the expiration of the initial 35 day period. The court can also grant a longer extension on request. A defendant can respond by doing any of the following:

Entering an Appearance

A defendant, or an attorney for the defendant, can enter an appearance in the case by returning the notarized acknowledgement of service to the plaintiff or by filing a general appearance with the court. A defendant who enters an appearance without filing an answer retains the option to contest some or all of the relief requested in the complaint at a later stage of the case.

Filing an Answer

A defendant can also enter an appearance in the case by filing an answer admitting or denying each allegation in the complaint.

Filing an Answer with a Counterclaim

Along with an answer, defendant can file a counterclaim, which is very similar to an original complaint, to assert the same or different grounds for divorce, or to seek affirmative relief from the court such as custody, alimony and/or child support. A spouse who chooses to file a counterclaim must include all of the supporting documents that would accompany a complaint. The purpose of a counterclaim is usually to ask the court to recognize that the defendant also has grounds for divorce and wants the case to go forward. If you are seeking affirmative relief from the court such as custody, alimony and/or child support, you are required to file a counterclaim.

Sometimes the reasons for filing a counterclaim are more psychological than tactical. A spouse who receives a complaint requesting a divorce on a fault-based ground may feel the need to present information demonstrating that the fault does not lie all on one side. While this is understandable, spouses filing counterclaims, like those filing initial complaints, should remember that escalation of conflict is rarely productive. If you are uncertain whether a counterclaim is necessary in your case, a consultation with an attorney can help you to decide.

A plaintiff will generally respond to a counterclaim with an answer admitting or denying each allegation of the counterclaim.

A Note about Default Judgments

If the defendant fails to answer the complaint for divorce within 35 days of service, the plaintiff can pursue a default judgment anytime within the next 6 months. In some cases, a spouse who has failed to answer a complaint will appear at the default hearing and ask to file an answer, or will even appear after entry of the default judgment with an explanation for the failure to appear earlier. If the defendant offers a good reason for the failure, the judge may reopen the case and allow defendant to file an answer, essentially turning the matter into a contested divorce case.

Chapter 6

Case Management

As soon as you and your spouse have filed your initial papers in the case, the court will begin to analyze the potential complexity of the case and employ various methods of case management, including assigning the case to one of four separate tracks and setting a case management conference (CMC).

New Jersey Court Rules provide that all civil family law cases, except for summary judgment matters, must follow one of four procedural tracks: priority, complex, expedited, or standard. The purpose of the track assignments is to streamline the court process so that pretrial and discovery matters proceed more efficiently. The different tracks allow the court to implement additional procedures with increased case management in more complex cases while shortening timelines and requiring earlier completion of certain phases in simpler cases. The court will assign your case to a track after each party has filed a Case Information Statement, or after a family court judge has held an initial CMC, whichever happens first.

Case Management Conference

The New Jersey Court Rule governing Case Management Conferences in civil family cases is Rule 5:5-7. Section (a) discusses priority and complex actions, and section (b) discusses standard and expedited cases. Regardless of the track assignment, the court will generally hold a CMC within 30 to 40 days of the expiration of time for filing the last responsive pleading. (The last responsive pleading will be either the defendant's answer to the initial complaint or the plaintiff's response to any answer and counterclaim filed by defendant.) In some cases more than one case management conference will be necessary, as the parties may need to spend substantial time during the early stages of the case narrowing down the issues in dispute.

The main purpose of the first case management conference is to set the schedule and parameters for pre-trial discovery. "Discovery" refers to the formal process used by attorneys for exchanging information in a case. Where a case appears to require substantial discovery, the judge often schedules future case management conferences to ensure that the case is moving along.

Case Track Assignments

The court will determine the most appropriate track for a specific case based on the number and type of contested issues in the case and the complexity of the applicable facts and law.

At the conclusion of the initial CMC, the judge will typically file a case management order setting out the basic timeline for the case, including a discovery schedule, and sometimes a tentative trial date. The schedule in the court's order must comply with the timelines dictated by the court rules for the applicable track.

If you and your spouse are both represented by attorneys, the judge making the case assignment will consider their input regarding the appropriate track assignment, but the final decision is up to the judge.

The court will sometimes reassign a case as it develops if the character of the case changes, and the parties can also request reassignment for appropriate reasons.

Priority

All cases involving contested custody or parenting time issues are assigned to the priority track. While such cases may be complicated, the courts put a very high premium on expediting resolution of matters affecting children. Family law judges must attempt to resolve all cases on the priority track within six months of the initial CMC. The judge assigned to the case will set a discovery schedule at the case management conference that allows completion within this time frame.

" After filing the Case Information Statement, the court will analyze your case and assign it to one of four tracks: priority, complex, expedited or standard. "

Bari Z. Weinberger, Esq.

Complex

Cases expected to require more time and more court and litigant resources than average are assigned to the complex track. Such cases generally have more parties, more claims or defenses, or greater factual or legal complexity. Cases in this track tend to have longer discovery timelines and proceed more slowly in general. Regardless of complexity, however, the Court Rules require a judge to hold an initial case management conference within 40 days after expiration of the deadline for filing the last responsive pleading in the case. The judge assigned to a complex case will set a reasonable discovery schedule at the initial CMC.

Expedited

Relatively simple cases that can be streamlined and promptly set for a final hearing or trial are assigned to the expedited track. These include cases where the parties have been married less than five years and have no children; cases where the parties have no disputes regarding income, value of assets, or custody and parenting time; cases where the spouses already have a property settlement agreement; and uncontested divorce cases. The initial case management conference in expedited cases must be held within 30 days after expiration of the deadline for filing the last responsive pleading, and the timeline for completion of discovery must not exceed 90 days from service of the original complaint.

Standard

All cases that do not qualify for one of the other tracks will be assigned to the standard track. Judges must hold an initial CMC in a case assigned to the standard track within 30 days after expiration of the deadline for filing the last responsive pleading. The discovery phase of standard track cases must be completed within 120 days from the date of service of the original complaint.

Chapter 7

Discovery

The amount of discovery that a divorce case will require depends on the complexity of a couple's financial status, and also on the degree to which both spouses are fully knowledgeable of such status and have access to financial records and information.

The discovery process in a New Jersey divorce case generally begins with the New Jersey Family Part Case Information Statement (CIS), which the court requires each spouse to file within 20 days following the defendant's answer or appearance.

The Case Information Statement

The CIS is a document containing detailed financial information. Although it can be very time consuming to fill out, taking the time and care to complete an accurate CIS is essential in a contested case and highly recommended even in the simplest uncontested case. If you are represented by an attorney, your attorney will help you complete the CIS; however, you are the only one who can provide accurate information. Parties must sign their CIS under penalty of perjury, must amend the CIS if there are any changes in the original information during the course of the case, and must be sure to file any amendments with the court no later than 20 days before a final hearing.

Your CIS provides the other party, the attorneys, and the judge with a snapshot of your income, assets and debts, the amount of money you need to live on each month, and any income available for support of minor children or the other spouse. If you are still negotiating settlement terms, the information in the CIS can provide the basis for calculation of any applicable child support as well as negotiation and structuring of alimony and equitable property distribution. You must include all of the following information in your CIS:

Personal Information:

In Part A of the CIS, you will need to provide detailed information about you and your family, including birth dates, marriage and separation dates, and a list of the outstanding issues in your case.

Employment and Income:

In Parts B and C, you will need to provide information about your employer, your annual income for the past year, your spouse's annual income for the past year, and your current year to date income. The information must be accurate and supported with pay stubs, W-2s and tax returns. You must also provide information about pay frequency and additional sources of income beyond base pay, including such things as stock options, bonuses, commissions, and any non-employment related income.

Monthly Expenses:

Part D of the CIS requires detailed information regarding monthly family expenses based on the marital standard of living, as well as current living expenses for couples who have already established separate residences. The former should reflect actual expenses of the marital lifestyle, and the latter should reflect actual current expenses for yourself and any children currently residing with you. While the amounts will necessarily include some estimates, it is important not to estimate too loosely and to provide exact figures whenever possible. If you are ever called upon to testify as to the figures you provide, you will have to have some proofs or basis for the numbers reflected in your budget. If you paid for most of your expenses with a credit card, debit card or by check, you should be able to compile estimates based on a review of your financial statements. Be sure to review statements for several months to obtain an average rather than relying on a single month, as expenses normally vary somewhat from month to month. Do not forget to include a monthly percentage for amounts paid annually or according to some other periodic schedule. To obtain a monthly figure for amounts paid weekly, multiply the amount by 4.3.

The purpose of the detailed budget is to help the parties and the court calculate whether or not the amount of available income is sufficient to meet each party's actual expenses. Sometimes when spouses physically separate and two households need to be maintained on the same amount of income that formerly supported one, they will have to liquidate and sell assets to make ends meet or tighten their respective belts. The CIS documents also help the parties and the court identify assets which may be available for sale and the probable proceeds that could be realized in this fashion.

After you have completed your budget, carefully evaluate whether or not the total amount makes sense in light of the money that you actually spent each month during your marriage or that you are actually spending now. If amounts seem to be missing, reconsider items you may have overlooked. Although the CIS form is broken down into categories to assist parties in identifying all usual and major expenses, it is still surprisingly easy to overlook minor expenses that may add up, or to underestimate the amount spent monthly on critical items such as groceries and household supplies.

Another common error is to estimate current expenses as an incorrect percentage of marital expenses. For example, expenses for three people living in the same house that four people formerly lived in would usually be significantly higher than three-fourths of the previous amount. Major expenses such as rent and mortgage are generally stable regardless of the number of people benefitting from the expenditure. Be sure to estimate actual expenses whenever possible rather than relying on percentages that may not be accurate.

Part D of the CIS requires completion of three separate schedules, as follows:

- **Shelter**. This category includes rental or mortgage payments, as well as payments for electricity, gas, water, sewer, telephone, cable, internet, homeowner's or renter's insurance, property taxes, repairs and maintenance, garbage and snow removal, landscaping charges, and any other monthly costs related to renting or owning your home.

- **Transportation**. This category includes monthly lease or loan payments on a car or other vehicle used for transportation, insurance premiums on any such vehicle, gasoline expenses, costs of repairs and maintenance, license and registration fees, commuter train or bus fare, and other costs related to transportation.

- **Personal Expenses**. Personal expenses include all of your other costs such as groceries, health insurance premiums, and unreimbursed expenses for medical, dental, or vision care, prescription drugs, and therapy or psychological counseling. You should also include payments to domestic employees or professionals such as accountants. If you and your spouse contributed on a regular basis to cash savings or retirement accounts, include these amounts as well. Be careful not to overlook items such as gift and entertainment expenses (including but not limited to birthday gifts, holiday gifts, special occasions), vacation costs, and the costs of personal services such as hair care. Monthly personal expenses also include child related costs such as babysitting or day care costs, private school tuition, camp fees, club dues, and any costs associated with sports, hobbies, or lessons. Include any support obligations you may have from previous relationships in your personal expenses as well.

Assets and Liabilities:

Part E of the CIS requires you to identify your marital and separate assets and liabilities. You must provide information regarding all existing checking and savings accounts, real estate holdings, timeshares, IRAs, pensions, Keoghs, ESOPs, SEPs, SSPs, 403b or 401k plans, mutual funds, stocks and bonds, and other investments. You will also need to include a detailed description of any leased or owned vehicle, including the year, make, model, value, and name listed on the title. Any business interests, collectables, or other personal property with significant value should be itemized in Part E. If you or your spouse has a whole life insurance policy with cash value, list the current cash value as of the date you complete your CIS.

In the liabilities section of Part E, provide information regarding any real estate mortgages, lines of credit, long-term debts such as student loans, revolving charges such as credit cards, short-term debts for items such as financed purchases or medical bills, and any contingent liabilities. You must specify the total amount due and the due date as well as the monthly payment. If you owe money to family members, friends or business colleagues, make sure to include information about these debts as well, so that the obligation will be taken into account during the equitable distribution in the case.

Special Issues:

In Part F, you should identify any special problems or challenges that you have not already addressed elsewhere in the CIS, if these are likely to have an impact on the case. For example, if you will need a forensic accountant to value a family business or you have a child with special needs, you should make a note of such circumstances in Schedule F.

Attachments:

Part G provides a checklist of required attachments such as W-2 forms, pay stubs and tax returns. Review this to ensure that you have provided all necessary supporting documents.

For more information about the Case Information Statement and how it is used in the New Jersey divorce process, see "New Jersey Case Information Statement Explained," by Bari Z. Weinberger, Esq. on the Weinberger Law Group website: http://bit.ly/divorce-cis.

" The CIS provides a snapshot of your income, assets, debts, and income available for the support of your children or spouse. "

Bari Z. Weinberger, Esq.

Basic Discovery Tools

After you and your spouse have completed and exchanged your CIS documents, you or your attorneys will analyze the information and evaluate the need to obtain additional information through follow-up discovery. Discovery tools often employed at this stage include:

- **Interrogatories**. Written questions requiring the opposing party to submit written answers under oath,

- **Requests for Production of Documents.** Written demands for documents such as bank statements, credit card statements, retirement account statements, etc., required to support claims in a case,

- **Requests for Admissions**. Written questions requiring the opposing party to either admit or deny the truth of alleged facts, and

- **Depositions**. Sworn oral testimony of a party, witness, or expert in a case, taken by an attorney out of court and recorded by a stenographer.

When to Use Basic Discovery Tools

Often one spouse in a divorce case has little knowledge of the couple's financial status, usually because the other spouse has typically handled such matters. Family law attorneys frequently use interrogatories and requests for production of documents in this type of situation to require the spouse with greater knowledge and access to information to answer extensive questions about relevant issues in a case and provide documents to support the answers, including such items as bank statements, cancelled checks, real estate sales contracts, partnership agreements, credit card statements, loan applications, tax returns, and other financial records. The list of necessary documentation may be voluminous.

Sometimes the answers to the initial set of interrogatories and the documents produced will provide all or most of the information necessary to clarify the financial picture. In other cases, follow-up questions and requests for additional documents will be necessary. When the answers to interrogatories and the documents produced fail to provide information adequate to allow a party to engage in meaningful settlement negotiations or prepare effectively for trial, a demand for more specific information or even depositions may be required. The attorney for one spouse may depose the other spouse, or in some cases, may depose an expert with specialized knowledge to obtain additional information or an explanation of information previously provided.

Additional Discovery Tools

There are many functions of discovery beyond the basic tools. Obtaining records from third party sources may require the use of subpoenas. In some cases, the value of real estate, a pension, or a business or professional practice can only be accurately determined through a professional appraisal or valuation. Parties sometimes want to have their spouse undergo a vocational evaluation to determine whether or not the spouse is working up to ability or should be imputed with income for the purpose of calculating spousal or child support. In cases where the parents are in disagreement over child custody, a psychological evaluation of one or more family members may be appropriate.

Parties with complex cases must understand that many levels of discovery may be required to collect sufficient information. While it is essential to have as complete a picture of a situation as possible in order to facilitate informed negotiation and settlement or prepare adequately for presentation of a case in court, when discovery is anticipated to be particularly long and complex, it is also critical for parties to balance their expectations of eventual recovery against the cost of the discovery process. Discovery is not only financially expensive; it can be emotionally draining, because of its adversarial nature. Where the additional information gathered in discovery is not likely to result in a significant improvement in results, moving toward settlement as rapidly as possible is usually a better course of action than continuing to expend family resources in court processes.

Chapter 8

Other Pre-Trial Procedures

Both during and after conclusion of the discovery phase of a case, there are several court procedures available to help parties move their disputes forward and either settle the case or prepare more effectively for trial. Some of these procedures are mandatory for parties faced with certain situations. Others are available but not required.

Both the procedures and the rules parties must follow in complying with procedures will vary slightly depending on the county in which a case has been filed. The following are available in some form in all New Jersey courts:

Child Custody and Visitation Dispute Resolution Procedures

All parents going through a New Jersey divorce in which a parenting-related issue is raised in the complaint, answer, or counterclaim are required to complete a Parents' Education Program. Parents who are unable to agree on child custody and parenting time (also called visitation) early in the case must also participate in court-mandated mediation in an effort to resolve such issues prior to trial.

Parents' Education Program

If either party raises an issue about custody, parenting time, or child support, both parties (usually separately and on different dates) must attend an educational program designed to inform families about children's needs during the process of separation and divorce. Parties will be exempt from this requirement if there is a restraining order in effect between them. The court may also excuse parties for other good reasons. Each parent must pay a fee of small fee for the program at the time they file the initial complaint for divorce or other pleading unless they are entitled to a fee waiver for financial reasons. If a parent who has not been excused from the program fails to attend, the court will consider this failure when determining custody or visitation.

Child Custody and Visitation Mediation

If parties identify a dispute about child custody or parenting time on the initial Case Management Order discussed above, the court will send the parties to mediation soon after the commencement of their case, unless the judge or the mediator exempts the case from this requirement due to the existence of circumstances such as domestic violence. Parents attend an orientation session and one or more mediation sessions without attorneys, and a court appointed mediator attempts to assist them in reaching a mutual agreement on custody and parenting.

Economic Dispute Resolution Procedures

Parties who have disputes regarding economic matters such as property distribution or payment of spousal support must also go through several procedures designed to help them resolve issues prior to trial, including the following:

Matrimonial Early Settlement Panel (MESP)

If the parties have not already reached settlement of all financial issues in the case, including alimony, child support, property division and counsel fees, the court will almost always assign the case to an early settlement panel for recommendations regarding resolution of financial issues. The New Jersey Court Rule governing county establishment of Early Settlement Programs, and party participation in such programs in appropriate cases, is Rule 5:5-5.

Parties with custody or visitation disputes must first participate in mediation to address parenting issues as these issues are not addressed at MESP. Settlement panels consist of volunteer attorneys with experience in family law in the county in which your case is scheduled. Parties generally submit materials such as position statements and copies of their case information statements to the panel prior to participating. If parties are represented by attorneys, the attorneys present arguments to the panel. Panel sessions are typically brief, usually lasting for no more than an hour or so, and parties generally attend only one panel session. Following the case presentations, the panel will make recommendations for resolving your case based on estimates of results that would be likely to follow a trial. Panel recommendations are not binding on the parties but will often help them to achieve a resolution or at least make some progress. If the parties agree with the recommendations of the panel, then they may get divorced while in court that very day.

> *For more information, please see: "Understanding the Early Settlement Panel", by Bari Z. Weinberger, Esq. (http://bit.ly/early-settlement).*

Economic Dispute Resolution

If the parties do not agree to a settlement on the basis of the early settlement panel recommendations, the court will generally assign the case to economic mediation. You and your attorneys will choose a mutually acceptable economic mediator and participate in economic dispute resolution for a minimum of two hours. The New Jersey Court Rule governing county establishment of post-MESP dispute resolution is Rule 5:5-6.

" File a motion for
temporary relief of
monthly expenses
or child custody
schedules at the
same time as your
divorce complaint. "

Bari Z. Weinberger, Esq.

Intensive Settlement Conference (ISC)

If all previous efforts at settlement have failed, the judge assigned to your case will conduct an informal settlement conference with you and your attorneys in a final effort to help you reach agreement before proceeding to trial. This is an intensive conference that usually lasts all-day.

Private Alternative Dispute Resolution

In addition to the dispute resolution processes required by the court, parties are free at any time to engage in private dispute resolution. The most commonly chosen form of alternative dispute resolution in divorce is mediation, however arbitration is another option. In mediation, a third party (the mediator) helps you to reach your own resolutions to your issues. In arbitration, the third party (the arbitrator) acts as a private judge in a streamlined and simplified version of a trial.

Motions for *Pendente Lite* Orders

Judges will often order temporary (or "*pendente lite*," which is a Latin term meaning "while the litigation is pending") relief during the pendency of a family law case. Because parties usually separate physically either before or during their divorce, one spouse is often left without the ability to pay expenses such as housing and monthly bills. Parties with disagreements about child custody, parenting schedules or child support payments cannot wait until the final outcome of a case before making arrangements. While many parents are able to work together cooperatively to maintain stability for the children during the separation process, others are less successful. Parents who disagree with one another strongly about these issues often need the court to order a temporary plan to prevent a high degree of disruption from negatively affecting the children. Sometimes a court will also award one spouse counsel fees in a *pendente lite* order. This is most likely to occur when the financial resources of one party are much greater than the other, leaving the less well-off spouse with very limited ability to participate in the case without financial assistance. In still other cases, one spouse may wish to have an order restraining the other spouse from spending, selling or encumbering certain assets.

Parties usually obtain *pendente lite* orders from the court through a notice of motion procedure which requires knowledge of both the law and the rules of court and is difficult to execute properly without competent attorney advice and assistance. Since courts want to ensure that each party has a chance to respond in writing to the other party's statements and arguments, there are strict time lines that apply to motions. In some emergency situations, the court may allow a party to give shorter notice to the other side and may grant relief "*ex parte*" before having a full hearing on the motion.

The most important document to present with a *pendente lite* motion for alimony or child support is the CIS. If you are filing or opposing a *pendente lite* alimony or support motion, it is important that you have a good understanding of all the financial documents supporting the CIS. For example, you must make sure that you understand all payroll deductions affecting your pay or your spouse's pay, as well as all types of income, deductions, exemptions or credits appearing on your tax returns. This may require consultation with an accountant, or with an individual from your human resources or payroll department.

Preservation of the Status Quo

The legal considerations courts take into account in evaluating requests for both temporary and permanent orders of alimony and child support are discussed in more detail in our companion e-books addressing substantive matters of law. Child support calculations follow very specific guidelines, while spousal support calculations require analysis of statutory factors. As a general rule, however, the purpose of *pendente lite* orders is to maintain the parties in the positions they were in before the commencement of the case. This means that a dependent or lower earning spouse will often be entitled to financial support from a higher earning spouse, and that to the extent possible, neither spouse should have to deviate significantly from the standard of living experienced during the marriage.

The status quo concept also extends to living arrangements for children. Courts make custody and parenting-time decisions on the basis of the children's best interests. One of those interests is in having routines disrupted as little as possible during the pendency of a divorce. Courts also consider it in the children's best interests to have frequent and continuing contact with both parents and to have both parents share in the responsibility of child rearing. What this means in the context of a *pendente lite* order is that the court may attempt to mimic a preexisting caretaking arrangement as closely as possible.

If you are bringing a motion for temporary sole or primary child custody, you should focus on convincing the court that you have been the primary or exclusive caretaker, or that there is some other overwhelming reason that you would be able to provide the children with a more stable environment than the other parent. If you have not been the primary caretaker, but you would like to have joint custody or liberal visitation, you should focus on showing the court that you have been actively involved in parenting and that it is in your children's best interests to have you continue in that role. Child custody matters can be complicated. You can find more information in our companion e-book entitled "Child Custody and Parenting Plans."

While there will be less evidence available at the *pendente lite* stage, the more accurate and complete evidence a party can present at this stage the better. Temporary court orders sometimes remain in effect for a substantial period of time and can have a potentially profound impact on the eventual outcome of a case. If you are in need of immediate financial relief or are having a custody or visitation dispute that cannot wait for resolution, you should contact an attorney as soon as possible. Your chances of a positive outcome will be higher with competent and experienced professional help.

Modification of *Pendente Lite* Orders

Pendente lite orders are, by their very nature, temporary. They are often based on less than full information due to the urgency of the situations at issue. For this reason they are subject to change at a trial or a later hearing date.

Practical Tip: Do Not Hesitate To Ask For Temporary Relief From The Court.

If you are having trouble establishing a custody schedule for your children, if you are struggling to pay your monthly living expenses because your spouse has withdrawn support, if you need help with legal fees, or if you have another issue requiring urgent attention, you can file a motion for temporary orders at the same time that you file your divorce complaint. If you believe your situation is an emergency, contact an attorney to find out how to get your issues heard as soon as possible.

Settling Your Contested Case Prior to Trial

Through a combination of court procedures and private alternatives, the great majority of spouses are able to work through their differences and reach settlement prior to trial, essentially transforming their case from a contested divorce to an uncontested divorce. If you and your spouse settle all of your issues, your attorneys can prepare a Marital Settlement Agreement, and your divorce can be finalized with a simple uncontested divorce hearing.

You can find more detailed information about uncontested divorce on the Weinberger Law Group website: http://bit.ly/uncontested.

Chapter 9

Family Law Trials

If you and your spouse have not succeeded in working out all issues in your case and you have exhausted all possibilities for negotiation and alternative dispute resolution, a judge will decide any remaining issues at trial. While the idea of a trial can cause a lot of anxiety, knowing what to expect may alleviate many of your concerns.

Attorney assistance is extremely important at the trial stage of a case. While some people do proceed through trial without an attorney, it is almost never a good idea and can result in serious adverse court decisions. Attorneys are trained in trial procedures, and a good attorney will understand the critical nuances of law that can make or break a court case.

Depending on how many issues remain to be resolved, a divorce or custody trial can take anywhere from a single day to several weeks, which may be spaced out over a number of months. In most states, including New Jersey, family law trials take place before a judge only (except in the rare case where a party may have the option of pursuing a jury trial due to the existence of an issue concerning a "marital tort"). At the trial, you and your spouse will each be permitted to present evidence, such as:

- your own testimony,
- witness/expert testimony,
- documents,
- pictures, and
- audio or video recordings.

Your attorney will keep your documents organized and help you prepare the evidence you need to succeed in your case. Be sure to follow your attorney's instructions regarding any items that you might need to bring to court yourself. Critical documents in your divorce file include the complaint, any counter complaint and answer, all supporting certifications, copies of any documents you may have obtained through discovery, and an up-to-date CIS. While the judge will have access to the case file, having your documents at hand in trial binders and being thoroughly familiar with them will be necessary for formal presentation purposes, will speed things up, and will give the judge the impression that you are a competent and credible person.

The evidence you need to present will depend on what you are attempting to convince the court of during the trial. If the judge will be making a decision on property division, be sure that you have financial information and title documents for the property. If alimony is an issue, you will need to present evidence on the marital standard of living as well as each party's income and expenses, including documents like pay stubs, tax returns and other proof of expenses and earnings. If the court will be deciding child custody and visitation, you may need witnesses who can testify regarding your child's needs and describe how you and your spouse allocated child-care prior to the divorce case, as well as how you have been handling things since the separation.

Trial Witnesses
Issuing Subpoenas:

A subpoena for purposes of trial is a document directing a witness to appear in court to testify. Once your case has been scheduled for a trial, the law gives you (or your attorney) the authority to serve a subpoena under the name of the clerk of the court on any witness that you will need to testify on your behalf. The best approach in preparing for trial is to subpoena every witness. If the witness is a friend or relative that you know is willing to testify, an official order like this may seem excessive, but even the most cooperative witness may have a timing conflict or may need to show an employer the subpoena to make sure that they get the time off from work.

If a witness has control over certain documents that you need to support your case, the subpoena can include a demand that the witness bring the documents to court. Subpoenas must be properly served. Anyone 18 or older can serve a subpoena requiring a witness to appear in family court by delivering a copy to the witness. You must complete service of all of your subpoenas at least five days before your trial date.

Witness Testimony:

Your attorney will review your testimony with you thoroughly prior to the trial and will also interview your witnesses so that they will understand what kind of questions to expect. You will need to present all of the facts that support your claims and make sure that all of the necessary documents are introduced into evidence. By the time a case is ready to go to trial, you and your spouse will have exchanged a great deal of written information, trial binders of exhibits, trial briefs, etc. It is important that you testify honestly and that your answers are consistent with the information already provided. If you or any of your witnesses have submitted to a deposition in the case, you need to be sure that you do not contradict anything you previously stated. If you absolutely must contradict something, be sure that you have a good explanation for the contradiction.

You can find more information about witness testimony and trial mechanics later in this book.

" If you and your spouse cannot work out all issues in your case, a judge will decide the remaining issues at trial. "

Bari Z. Weinberger, Esq.

Using Expert Witnesses

If an issue at trial requires an expert opinion, both you and your spouse will generally be aware of this well in advance. Courts require expert testimony concerning any subject commonly considered to be beyond the normal knowledge of a non-professional person. Experts often provide written reports containing recommendations for settlement purposes prior to trial. If a trial appears likely, the attorneys may also want to depose the other spouse's expert witnesses so that they will know how best to cross-examine them at the trial.

Expert witnesses are usually highly paid professionals and are expensive to retain. Having an expert appear at trial can be particularly costly, as you may have to pay the expert for a half-day, a full-day or several days of time, most of which the witness will probably spend waiting to testify.

New Jersey Court Rules permit parties in family law cases to hire either individual or joint experts. The court can also appoint experts independently, regardless of whether or not the parties have already retained their own. A judge who appoints an expert should specify very clearly what the expert will be doing and what the scope of the expert's opinion will be. If the parties hire a joint expert or the court appoints an expert, the parties will usually share the costs. The court may order them to split costs equally or may order the party with greater economic means to pay a higher percentage of the cost, pending possible adjustment at trial.

While hiring an expert can sometimes be critical to a case, your attorney can help you reduce the costs involved in using experts by advising you whether a joint opinion on a matter is likely to suffice or whether you need to hire an independent expert. In many cases a court will give more credibility to a joint or court-appointed expert, as that expert is neutral to the parties and has no motivation to present only the aspects of a case favorable to the party paying for the opinion. Experts in some fields can also gain a reputation for commonly representing either one side or the other of an issue. Judges get to know these experts and will often know what they are likely to say before they even say it. On the other hand, if your spouse has retained an expert who will be providing the court with an opinion that is against your interests, you may need to hire your own expert to contradict this event. Your attorney can help you to find a reputable expert whose opinion a judge will likely respect.

Court-appointed experts conduct independent investigations. Parties must cooperate with such investigations but are entitled to have their attorneys and their own experts present during any kind of examination by a court-appointed expert. Experts are not permitted to communicate with the court "ex parte," meaning that the parties will have prior notice of any communication between the expert and the judge and can be present with their attorneys during any such communication. Court-appointed experts must submit any findings or reports to both parties as well as to the court. Any party who is not happy with an expert's opinion can submit reports from their own experts as well as take a deposition of the court's expert. Judges are not supposed to assume that an expert they have appointed is automatically more believable than an expert hired by either party, and court-appointed experts are subject to the same cross-examination as any other expert.

The following are the general categories of experts that courts or parties most often hire as witnesses in family law cases:

Medical, Mental Health or Social Experts: A medical, mental health or social expert opinion might be required in several different situations. One of the most common is where one party is claiming an inability to work or to be fully employed due to a medical or mental health issue. Another common situation is where one parent is trying to demonstrate that the other parent has a serious health issue that impacts parenting ability, such as a substance abuse problem or a personality disorder. This can be part of an overall custody evaluation (see below). Medical, mental health or social experts can be physicians, psychiatrists, psychologists, occupational therapists, or other health professionals. Therapists who are treating any member of the family cannot be called by the court as expert witnesses.

The expert may want to conduct an independent medical examination or perform psychological testing. This cannot occur without your consent. If your spouse's expert or the court's expert wishes to conduct any kind of examination, be sure to discuss this thoroughly with your attorney ahead of time.

The court can also order a representative of the family division to conduct a social investigation and "Best Interest Report" to help the judge make the custody determination and parenting time arrangements that ensure that the best interest of the child(ren) are met. This is especially likely to occur in a case where there is a lot of conflict in the family and the parents are unable to agree on a custody arrangement, but neither spouse has the financial means to fund a custody evaluation.

Child Custody or Parenting Experts: Child custody evaluations are performed by mental health experts. Regardless of whether or not a party engages this type of expert or the court appoints one, the expert will be held to a very high standard of neutrality and must base any opinion on the best interests of the children involved. The expert can consider any information pertinent to the case but must specifically consider the criteria set forth in the child custody provisions of the New Jersey statutes (N.J.S.A. 9:2-4) and must reference those criteria in any reports.

If you are going to trial on a child custody issue, you will probably need the opinion of a child custody evaluator. Judges rely heavily on such professional opinions. Parents should be aware, however, that the science behind custody evaluations is not by any means foolproof. Judges rely on them primarily because they are often the best means available of making sense out of conflicting stories between parents. A custody evaluator has the benefit of professional wisdom, but does not have a crystal ball that guarantees the best decision, and cannot necessarily do a better job in determining the best interests of any particular child than the child's own parents can.

Since child custody evaluations and trials are extremely expensive, particularly if more than one evaluation is involved, going to trial on a custody issue involves spending a great deal of money for a result that will not necessarily be any better after the expense. Even more troubling, custody evaluations are invasive and often increase family conflict due to the heightened anxiety experienced by everyone in the family. You should discuss the necessity and utility of using a custody evaluator in depth with your attorney. If the evaluation seems inevitable, it is absolutely critical to obtain a skilled evaluator who will keep your children's interest at the forefront. Your attorney should be aware of the reputations of different evaluators in the community and can advise you regarding the best way to select an evaluator.

The evaluator will meet with all of the family members; usually each parent will meet the evaluator with the children. The evaluator may also meet with family members individually and will sometimes meet with other people as well, such as teachers, physicians, or extended family members. Sometimes the evaluator will perform psychological tests.

If you are going through a custody evaluation, your attorney will give you information to help you prepare. While the experience can be intimidating, you should try to act as naturally as possible. If the court has given instructions on what the children should be told in advance, follow the instructions exactly. If the court has not given instructions, ask your attorney for advice on how to proceed. Do not ever try to "prep" children to give rehearsed statements or to say negative things about the other parent. These tactics are likely to backfire under the scrutiny of an experienced mental health professional.

If there is a home visit, be sure that your home is neat and clean and that places for children to sleep, play and do school work are well-maintained. Otherwise, do not obsess about having the perfect home or being the perfect parent. An evaluator will be primarily concerned with observing the long-standing relationship that exists between you and your children.

Economic Experts: Economic experts include real estate and business appraisers. They can also include forensic accountants who can evaluate pensions or other financial assets and give opinions on the various tax ramifications of your divorce and lifestyle/real income. Vocational examiners are a type of economic expert qualified to give an opinion on job opportunities and probable income for particular jobs or professions in the area. One spouse may ask a vocational examiner to give an opinion to support a claim that the other spouse is either voluntarily unemployed or underemployed.

Real Estate Valuations: You may need to know the value of your home or another property so that you can give it the appropriate weight in the equitable distribution of your assets. If you are planning to sell the property and divide the proceeds 50/50 you probably do not need an appraisal, although you might still need a rough estimate of the value if the amount impacts another issue, such as the need for alimony for example. If you are planning on listing the property or trying to decide whether or not one of you should keep it, a realtor can give you a fair estimate of value through a comparative market analysis. Realtors have sometimes been known to estimate values higher rather than lower, in the hopes of getting the listing. If you rely on a realtor's opinion, be sure to look at the comparable recent sales in the neighborhood and make your own honest evaluation of how your property compares to these. A professional real estate appraiser will make a more precise evaluation by performing a home inspection and comparing the specifics of your home to other homes recently sold in the area. Professional real estate appraisals are relatively inexpensive. If one party will be keeping the home, it will usually be worth the cost of obtaining an accurate valuation. Note that if valuation of the real estate will be an issue at trial, appraisals are evidential at court, whereas a comparative market analysis by a realtor is not.

Valuing Pensions and Other Financial Assets: While the valuation of financial assets can be quite complex, the acceptable methods of valuation are fairly standardized. Most deferred compensation plans have a face value that is easy to determine. Many pension plans, on the other hand, require an analysis to determine present and future value, which may depend on different variables. An actuarial financial expert can perform this analysis and can also give information regarding the tax implications of dividing assets, and what the difference in tax treatments might be depending on when an asset is distributed.

Your attorney can help you decide what kind of an expert you need for these types of assets. Provided that you and your spouse can agree on someone who is qualified, experienced, and neutral, a joint expert will often be a good economic choice. Depending on the type of asset involved, you may also need an expert to prepare a Qualified Domestic Relations Order (QDRO) to ensure that the asset is properly distributed.

Business Valuations: The value of a family business is frequently subject to some degree of equitable distribution in divorce, even where one spouse owned and operated the business before the marriage. A court will generally try to award the business to the spouse who is most involved in running it, while awarding the other spouse compensatory value.

Business valuations can sometimes vary considerably from evaluator to evaluator, due to the difficulty in placing an exact dollar amount on certain aspects, particularly goodwill. Whether you plan to hire your own expert or obtain a joint expert with your spouse, make sure that you have a good understanding of the types of valuations the expert has performed in the past. If you have been operating the business yourself, you may have your own legitimate expert opinion regarding the value, but it is unlikely that your spouse will simply accept your opinion, as you may have a motivation to undervalue the business if you believe the asset will go to you in the distribution. On the other hand, you will not want to accept any expert your spouse's attorney proposes without an independent review of the expert's qualifications and potential biases, as your spouse may have a motivation to try to inflate the value of the business. (Of course, if your spouse is the manager and expects to receive the business in the distribution, your respective motivations will be reversed.) If you know of professionals in your field that would be qualified to express an opinion regarding the business's value, be sure to let your attorney know. Your professional knowledge could be valuable.

Business valuations can be sensitive matters, as they require turning over the books and records of the business to a stranger, and in some cases, allowing that person to inspect the workplace. Under certain circumstances, you may be able to claim that some records are privileged. Your attorney can provide you with advice on this aspect of the valuation. You can ask the court for permission to redact (black out) confidential client information or obtain a protective order, but in general, you will have to produce everything that the expert needs to form a well-reasoned opinion.

Valuing Other Assets: Depending on your exact situation, you may need to obtain a formal appraisal of other assets, such as antiques or artwork. Your attorney can help you decide whether or not an appraisal is necessary and if so what kind of an appraiser to use.

Trial Mechanics

As previously noted, the overwhelming majority of divorce cases are resolved at some point prior to trial. If you are in the unfortunate minority of couples whose case reaches the trial stage, it can be helpful to understand how the process works. There can be some significant differences in the ways that courts conduct family law trials from state to state, and even within states, every courtroom is slightly different; nevertheless, the general format of a family law trial will be similar regardless of where it takes place.

Even if your case does settle prior to a full trial, you may find that one or more issues in your case require a "plenary" (complete) hearing. This can occur prior to the end of the case, or even after the divorce judgment is final. Common situations requiring plenary hearing after divorce include spousal support modifications and relocation custody cases. Plenary hearings follow a format similar to a traditional trial.

Presenting witnesses and documentary evidence correctly at trial requires following the rules of evidence, as well as all state and county court rules. These rules can be quite technical and challenging to understand without attorney assistance.

Pre-Trial Matters

There are many court procedures that you will need to go through prior to your case being set for a trial. These are detailed earlier in this chapter. Once you have a trial date, many judges will ask you and your spouse (or your attorneys) to submit a number of things prior to the trial. These generally include a trial brief that explains each party's overall position and summarizes the supporting law and facts, witness and exhibit lists, and any stipulations (agreements regarding specific facts) that parties have reached in advance. Some judges will also ask for advance copies of any exhibits either party intends to introduce into evidence.

> **Practical Tip: Make A Good Courtroom Impression.**
> While it is not necessary to buy a suit or an expensive dress if you do not already own these items, the more pulled together and professional you appear in court, the more likely the judge is to take you seriously. Avoid sweat pants, t-shirts and any clothing that could possibly be seen as provocative (tank tops, super tight pants, very short skirts, etc.), as well as any unduly attention grabbing clothing (odd hats or excessive jewelry, for example). Make sure that whatever you wear is clean and neatly pressed, without rips, stains or hanging hemlines. Be courteous and polite to everyone in the courtroom. Stand up when the judge enters the courtroom. Do not ever blurt statements out in court while someone else is speaking.

What to Expect in the Courtroom

Court security—In all likelihood, when you enter the courthouse you will have to go through a security check similar to an airport security check. Your bags will be x-rayed and you will not be permitted to bring in any weapons or sharp objects.

Court personnel—Depending on the nature of your court proceedings, in addition to the judge hearing your case, you may encounter several other court personnel. These may include a court clerk, who is responsible for posting case lists and checking parties in and recording the proceedings; a law clerk, who handles calendar and motion matters; and a sheriff's officer.

Case Presentation

The spouse who filed the original complaint in divorce will be the plaintiff and the other spouse will be the defendant. The plaintiff will present evidence first, then the defendant, and then the plaintiff will have a chance to rebut the defendant's case. Before either party begins to present evidence, there may be a pre-trial conference during which the judge will assess which matters are still at issue and make one last effort at encouraging the parties to settle. Immediately before the parties start to present their witnesses, the judge will usually ask for opening statements from each side. These statements summarize the evidence each party plans to present in support of the case. If the parties have presented trial briefs, opening statements may be waived or may consist of just a few summarizing and clarifying remarks.

The plaintiff will call witnesses first and examine them through direct questioning. Direct questioning requires the use of open-ended questions, rather than leading questions that may suggest the answer and require only a yes or no response. While you may be used to seeing attorneys use leading questions on television or in the movies, in a formal court proceeding leading questions are only allowed on cross-examination or with the judge's permission if a witness turns out to be unexpectedly "hostile" (this does not necessarily mean angry, just deliberately unhelpful).

The questions your own attorney asks you will not be a surprise, as the attorney will practice questions and answers with you and with other helpful witnesses in advance. Your attorney should also provide you with information about cross-examination and practice this technique with you as well so that you will know what kind of testimony is appropriate and how to phrase your answers.

You will get a chance to tell your whole story on direct examination. It is important to understand that your testimony should only answer the questions your attorney asks you. The judge will have little patience for listening to extraneous information that does not address the topic under review. Sometimes a judge who needs clarification will ask some questions as well. You must cover all of the critical information during the initial direct exam, as any further questioning following cross-exam is limited to issues already raised.

The defendant will be able to cross-examine the plaintiff's witnesses, and then the plaintiff's attorney can ask some follow up questions if necessary to correct any mistaken impressions resulting from the cross-exam. Occasionally a family law plaintiff's attorney will call the other spouse or one of the other spouse's witnesses as part of the plaintiff's case. This may be necessary to establish certain information, and it can even be tactically useful as it tends to throw the other side off balance, but it can also make it easier for the other side to present a case, as the defendant's attorney can then cross-examine the defendant or the defendant's witness. The important documents and other exhibits in the case will be incorporated into the testimony, and the attorney will ask the court to admit the exhibits into evidence as the witnesses address them.

After the plaintiff has presented all witnesses and introduced all evidence, the defendant will proceed to introduce direct testimony and exhibits in the same manner. There may be some exceptions to the planned order of witnesses due to schedules. This is particularly common with experts who have very busy schedules. Parties often wish to have their experts testify as soon as they are available to prevent escalation of fees while the expert is waiting for a turn. Occasionally a court will even allow the defendant's attorney to conduct direct examination of a witness during the plaintiff's case, or vice versa. After the defendant has completed putting on the case, the plaintiff can present a "rebuttal" case. This is a chance to respond to any new topics the defendant raised; a plaintiff cannot rehash old ground or introduce new issues at this point.

Closing arguments or "summations" follow the rebuttal. During the closing arguments the attorneys will summarize the facts presented and make arguments as to why such facts support each claim in the case. Judges allow varying amounts of time for summations. While they do not want to cut the attorneys' time too short, the crowded schedule in most family law courtrooms necessitates imposing some limits. Sometimes, a summation will be permitted in writing.

It is important to be prepared for the disconcerting effect of the congested family law calendar, which often results in the constant interruption of an on-going trial. Rather than putting on a five day case in one week, for example, the case could be broken up into one or two days per week for a month, or even extended over a longer period of time. You may also have to wait weeks or even months for the court's decision. Once you have the trial court's decision, your case may be concluded once and for all, or one party may wish to appeal the decision or seek post-judgment relief. These options are discussed in more detail in the next chapter.

Issuing a Final Judgment of Divorce

After you have settled your case or completed a trial before a judge, the court will enter a final judgment of divorce ending your marriage and incorporating any settlement agreement or judicial orders for relief. If one of the parties has prepared and submitted a proposed order for the court, the judge may sign this order with or without making changes, or may prepare a new order. Often the judge will ask an attorney for one of the parties to prepare a new order. A party who prepares a proposed order must send the other side a copy, and that party will have five days to review the order and make any objections before the judge signs it.

Chapter 10

Motions for Reconsideration and Appeals

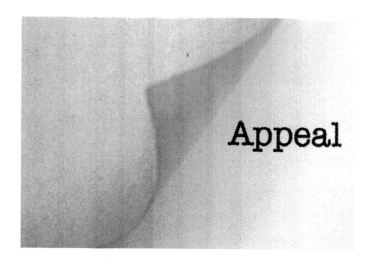

If you have been a party to a litigated family law matter that has gone all the way through a full hearing on an important issue, or a trial on all outstanding issues, and you have received a disappointing decision from the court, you may be wondering whether or not it makes any sense to keep on fighting.

Gearing up for a legal court battle often takes every ounce of a person's strength. Losing the battle is a terrible let down, and it is normal to feel dejected and emotionally drained. It is also normal to have trouble accepting the decision and to feel a strong urge to continue fighting.

Sometimes the impulse to carry on the fight is rational, but in many cases, it is a form of denial. Situations that justify putting additional time, money and emotional energy into a family law battle beyond the trial level are exceedingly rare, but that is not to say that they do not exist. If you find yourself in a situation where you need to assess your losses and decide what direction to take next, give yourself a few days to absorb the blow and regain some of your equilibrium, and then discuss the situation with your attorney.

If you decide that you want to move forward, you will have to act quickly. The available remedies are limited and must be pursued within strict time frames.

Motions for Rehearing or Reconsideration

After a hearing or a trial in a New Jersey family court case, either party can ask the court to consider additional evidence, amend findings of fact and conclusions of law, or make new findings and conclusions, and change the judgment or order in the case. Courts rarely grant such requests, however. Minor errors occur frequently during case presentations and most such errors are considered "harmless." Only errors that have a substantial impact on the rights of one of the parties justify reconsideration of the court's decision. It is not a process to merely take a second bite of the apple due to a disappointing result. You will need to present a legally appropriate application consistent with the court rules and case law to have any viable chance of success.

A party who files a motion requesting the court to reconsider a decision must ordinarily serve a notice of motion specifically describing the perceived error of fact or law within 20 days following service of the court's judgment or order on all parties to the case. The rest of the motion process will be conducted as a typical motion would be, with comparable response times for objections from the other side and a proper opportunity to submit a reply by the movant.

A party asking for reconsideration cannot ordinarily bring up a new issue or introduce new evidence that the trial court did not have the opportunity to consider but was available to submit had the applicant provided it the first time around. In some cases, however, a party can ask the court to vacate a judgment even after the 20 day reconsideration period has expired, based on the discovery of critical new evidence, or based on a few other limited reasons, including fraud, mistake, or excusable neglect. A judge who discovers a clerical error in a decision (a miscalculation of income available for support, for example) can correct the mistake at any time, whether a party brings it to the court's attention in a motion or not. If a party is asking the court to reconsider a decision or vacate a judgment based on the discovery of new evidence, the request must include information explaining why such evidence was impossible to produce during the original hearing or trial. These are very unusual kinds of situations. Neglecting to obtain complete evidence or to subpoena all necessary witnesses before a hearing will not normally constitute an adequate excuse for failing to provide the proof required in a case.

A family law judge with a busy calendar who has taken the time to read detailed briefs, review all evidence presented, listen to attorney arguments, and make specific findings of fact and law, is not likely to be favorably inclined toward granting a motion for reconsideration. Motions, trials and plenary hearings are time-consuming and expensive, and a judge will not be eager to take any action which would result in the duplication of costs, either for the court system or for the other party in the case, without an extremely good reason.

If a party indicates in a motion that a court has made insufficient or unclear findings of fact, the court might provide an expanded decision with additional specifics. Sometimes the expanded findings will help the party decide whether or not it is worth the time and expense to file an appeal.

Appeals

If you have gone through a motion, plenary hearing or trial and you are finding it difficult to accept the court's decision, you can consider seeking review of the decision by the appellate court. Be forewarned, however, that you will have a challenging road ahead of you. Family law appeals are unusual. Most cases settle before reaching the trial stage. Trial costs tend to be extremely high, and the costs of an appeal can be even higher. These costs include filing fees in the appellate court, fees for obtaining a trial court transcript, and fees of an attorney who has experience arguing family law appeals. In some cases, if you lose your case, you may even have to pay your former spouse's attorney's fees.

The appellate attorney will have to spend many hours reviewing the case file and court transcripts, researching the basis for the appeal, writing a detailed appellate brief to exacting court standards, and possibly, arguing the case before a two or three panel of judges. Appeals also tend to drag on in the courts; more often than not it will be more than a year before the court issues a decision. While New Jersey courts place some family appeals on an accelerated schedule, particularly those concerning matters of emergency such as issues of child custody, the time involved in going through the appeal process can still be substantial.

The time limits for filing appeals vary from state to state but are usually quite short; in some states parties have as little as 30 days from the date of a trial court's decision to notify the other party of the appeal. In a New Jersey family law case, a party has 45 days from the entry of a final judgment to file a notice of appeal, except in cases terminating parental rights, in which a party must file the notice within 21 days of the entry of judgment.

Appeals require strict adherence to specific requirements of form and timing. New Jersey courts require the appellant (the party who is appealing the decision) to include a Case Information Statement, a copy of the final judgment, and a certification that the appellant has ordered and paid for the trial court transcript with the notice of appeal. It is critical to have the assistance of an attorney who is familiar with all of the time-lines and procedures of the appellate court in your jurisdiction, as well as the legal aspects of the issue you wish to appeal. If you attempt to proceed without the help of a knowledgeable attorney, you will be risking a dismissal of your appeal on procedural grounds.

Immediately following a negative court decision, you may feel that all of this extra time, aggravation, and expense will be worth it; remember, however, that the chances of success on appeal are much, much lower than the chances of success at trial. Appellate judges give great deference to trial court decisions. In a family law case the trial court judge is the fact finder and often the ultimate arbiter of fairness as well; an appellate court will not ordinarily disturb any decision based on sufficiency or believability of evidence or on the trial court's discretionary judgment. The standard is whether or not a trial court judge abused his or her discretion in making the ultimate decision. This is difficult to establish, but not always impossible.

None of this information is intended to discourage you from pursuing an appeal if your heart, your mind, and most importantly, your legal counsel, are all telling you that it is the right thing to do. It is important, however, that you understand the stakes involved and that you be prepared for any potential outcome.

" If your litigated law matter has provided a disappointing final decision…think carefully, then discuss with an attorney. You have to act quickly due to strict time frames. "

Bari Z. Weinberger, Esq.

Errors Justifying Appellate Review:

A party cannot ordinarily bring up an issue on appeal for the first time and cannot introduce new evidence that the trial court did not have the opportunity to consider. Some reasons that might justify an appeal include a trial court's:

- failure to apply controlling statutory or case law or court rules correctly,
- failure to conduct a full hearing to resolve a material dispute between the parties, or
- abuse of discretion.

If the appellate court agrees with the appellant that one of these serious errors occurred, and that there is a good chance that the error had a significant effect on the result in the case, the court may reverse the decision of the trial court, or may request the trial court to take the case back for reconsideration and make further findings or conduct a new hearing.

Attorneys and judges sometimes refer to errors that neither party brings to the court's attention during the trial or that the appellate court takes notice of on its own after one party files an appeal as "plain" errors, while they refer to errors raised during trial as "harmful" errors. There are some legal distinctions between these two types of errors, and an appellate court might be more likely to consider an error serious if an attorney brought it to the trial court's attention when it occurred. In many cases, however, an appellate court can consider an error made during the trial even if neither party raises it during the trial or on appeal. If you believe that a serious error affected the decision in your case, you should discuss this with your attorney.

Regardless of when an error is brought to light or who brings it to the appellate court's attention, it will not normally justify a change in the decision on appeal unless it clearly could have led to an unjust result. If the result the trial court reached is reasonable and supported by sufficient credible evidence in the record, the appellate court will not disturb it. Only compelling circumstances justify an exception.

Requirement of Final Judgment or Court Permission:
In most cases, a party cannot file an appeal unless the trial court's order or judgment is final, meaning that it addresses and disposes of all remaining issues between all parties to a case. If the decision is not final, a party can bring a motion requesting permission to file an "interlocutory" (meaning during the case) appeal in the interests of justice. Courts ordinarily grant such requests only in cases of true emergency. This generally requires an appellant to demonstrate both a basis for the appeal that appears to have a good chance of success, and the existence of a strong possibility that irreparable harm will occur if the review has to wait to go through normal channels.

In a limited number of situations, the law automatically allows an interlocutory appeal. If your divorce case has been bifurcated (divided into separate issues) and you receive a final determination on the child custody part of your case, you do not have to wait for a decision on the rest of your case before appealing the custody decision. Normally, however, if the judge makes a decision on one aspect of your case pending a trial on the remaining issues, you will have to wait until after the trial to appeal the interlocutory decision.

Standard of Review:

In the majority of family law appeals, an appellate court will only be looking at whether or not the trial judge abused its discretion. While there must be credible evidence supporting the trial judge's decision, where the facts conflict, the judge is responsible for deciding which facts to believe and how much weight to give each fact.

For example, in a case involving the equitable distribution of property, the court would have to find sufficient credible evidence regarding the amount of assets to be divided and the value of the assets, but the decision about how to divide them between the spouses largely depends on what the judge believes to be fair. While the court is required to follow correct procedures and consider the factors listed in any applicable statute, as well as correctly apply any case law interpreting the statute, the relative weight to assign different factors is completely up to the judge.

Disposition of Appeals:

Appeals are usually considered by panels of two or three judges. Sometimes the court will ask for arguments from the attorneys. The court can reverse the trial court or can send the case back (remand it) for a new trial or for some other action. In the majority of cases, however, the appellate court will decide that the appeal has no merit and will affirm the decision of the trial court.

No matter how unfair you consider the trial court's decision, do not waste time and money filing an appeal unless you believe that all of the requirements for a successful appeal have been satisfied. Something to keep in mind while you are evaluating your chances of success on appeal is that regardless of how painful the trial court's decision may be, it at least has the benefit of finality. An appeal may accomplish nothing more than keeping painful feelings alive for an extended period of time. Accepting the court's decision, on the other hand, can often provide long-awaited closure. Talk candidly with your lawyer about the likelihood of success on appeal. While the odds of succeeding are usually small, we have the process in place for a reason: the lower court does not always get it right and a remedy is available through the appellate court to correct the error.

Chapter 11

Post-Judgment Motions

For many fortunate people, entry of a final divorce decree means that everything connected with the former marriage has been settled once and for all. For others, the divorce decree brings closure and the ability to move on, but does not remove the possibility that loose ends may need additional attention in the future.

A divorce case is unlike most other lawsuits in that even after the parties have resolved all issues and the judge has entered a final judgment, matters commonly arise that require the former spouses to engage in additional settlement negotiations or even appear in court. The majority of issues that arise post-divorce occur when:

- one party fails to carry out the orders of the court, or
- a change of circumstances justifies a modification of the court's orders.

The following is some basic information about each of these potential situations.

> *You can find out more about how New Jersey law applies to each of these situations by consulting our website sections on child custody and parenting, child support, and spousal support (alimony) at www.WeinbergerLawGroup.com.*

Motions to Enforce Litigant's Rights

When one party fails to follow the terms of a court order, the other party's primary remedy will be to file a motion to enforce litigant's rights. This type of motion allows a party to ask the court to enforce previous orders and impose penalties on the party failing to comply, including, when appropriate, monetary sanctions. In the family law context, one former spouse may use this type of motion to compel the other to pay child support or alimony, as well as comply with the terms of custody and visitation orders. New Jersey Court Rule 5:3-7 includes an explanation of special remedies that are available following violation of orders regarding parenting time, alimony, or support.

Enforcing Custody and Visitation Orders:

Parents have a legal duty to comply with court-ordered parenting plans. In most cases, this duty includes encouraging a child to spend time with the other parent. On the one hand, parents need to maintain a certain degree of flexibility to make a parenting plan work; running off to court after every minor violation of the terms of a plan is not conducive to a peaceful co-parenting relationship. On the other hand, consistent or extreme violations may be best addressed through legal channels.

If you find yourself in a situation where your child's other parent is consistently violating the court's orders regarding custody and visitation, you may want to bring both a motion to enforce litigant's rights and a motion requesting a change in the parenting arrangements. An attorney can help you decide which motion or motions would be necessary and appropriate.

Enforcing Payment of Child Support or Alimony:

A parent who is not receiving timely child support or alimony payments can also file a motion to enforce litigant's rights. The superior court has the authority to order a party responsible for paying child support or alimony to bring all payments up to date, make future payments on time, and pay any attorney's fees the recipient has incurred in bringing the motion. The courts also have various tools available for ensuring compliance with orders for enforcement.

Motions to Modify Existing Orders

The court entering a final judgment of divorce will maintain jurisdiction over all matters relating to parenting and child support until the children attain financial independence. The court also maintains jurisdiction over payment of alimony until a designated termination date, or indefinitely in the case of permanent alimony. This means that the court retains the power to make changes in child custody or visitation arrangements, as well as child support payments and alimony payments, whenever there is a substantial change in circumstances after entry of the initial orders. In general, courts will not modify orders post-judgment unless the change in circumstances has already occurred and is expected to continue indefinitely or for at least a considerable length of time.

Modifying Child Custody and Visitation Orders:

A parent applying for modification of custody or visitation must prove that circumstances have changed substantially since the date of the original decision. After an adequate showing of changed circumstances, a court will review the existing parenting orders in light of all factors relevant to the best interests of the child, just as in an original custody determination. Courts generally require parents to make their best efforts to work out an acceptable new plan through negotiation or mediation prior to bringing the matter to court.

" Be aware that post-divorce matters may arise that require former spouses to negotiate additional settlement items or even appear in court. "

Bari Z. Weinberger, Esq.

Modification or Termination of Alimony:

As a general rule, once a divorce is final and a couple has entered into a marital settlement agreement or a judge has ordered alimony payments, the amount and terms of payment are modifiable only if one spouse can show that circumstances have changed substantially and that the change is likely to be permanent. Other factors may also limit modifiability, including the type of alimony, the terms of the initial order, and the existence of any agreements between the parties regarding modification. Within the scope of these potential restrictions, a former spouse who is paying alimony can file a motion requesting a decrease or termination of the obligation, or a recipient can file a motion requesting an increase.

Most types of alimony will end if the recipient remarries or enters into a new civil union. The death of either spouse will also terminate the obligation. Other situations may or may not be a legitimate ground for a modification, depending on all of the circumstances. The most common reason people bring motions requesting a change in spousal support are an increase or decrease in either party's income.

Modifying or Terminating Child Support:

As with other post-judgment modifications, the initial burden of producing evidence that a change of circumstances has occurred is on the parent seeking the modification. Once a parent has provided initial evidence of circumstances justifying a change, the court will determine whether or not to hold a full hearing. The child support guidelines are subject to periodic administrative review and change, but a motion for an increase in support cannot be based only on the fact that there has been a change in the guidelines. There must be independent support for a change in the individual case.

The following are some common reasons people bring motions requesting a change in child support payments:

- an increase or decrease in either parent's income,
- a change in a child's needs,
- a change in parenting time,
- the birth of a new child,
- a child's emancipation (achievement of financial independence), or
- a child's enrollment in college.

Practical Tip: Do Not Put Off Addressing A Change Of Circumstance.

While a court will not address a change of circumstances claim until after the circumstances have actually occurred, once the new circumstances are in place, it is important to bring a claim promptly (with some specific exceptions). People who wait months or even years before seeking a modification of support will generally find themselves shut out from the possibility of receiving retroactive relief.

The initial burden of producing evidence that a change of circumstances has occurred is on the party seeking a modification. If the court is satisfied with this initial evidence, the parties will be permitted to engage in discovery regarding each other's full financial circumstances. If the court determines that sufficient evidence exists to hold a "plenary" (meaning full or complete) hearing, all of the factors involved in the original determination will apply to the modification.

Further Information and Resources:

- For an overview of the contested divorce process in New Jersey, see the Weinberger Law Group website: http://bit.ly/contested-divorce.

- The Court Rules governing practice in New Jersey state courts can be found at the New Jersey Courts website: http://bit.ly/court-rules. Rules specific to family law appear in Part V. The general rules in Part I also apply to family law cases. The rules governing civil actions in general appear in Part IV and apply to civil family law cases unless a more specific rule appears in Part V. The rules applicable to appeals in the New Jersey Supreme Court and the Appellate Division of the New Jersey Superior Court appear in Part II.

- Weinberger Law Group maintains a listing of all New Jersey courthouses, including directions and contact information as well as additional helpful information relating to each individual New Jersey county. You can access this information on the Weinberger Law Group website: http://bit.ly/nj-courts.

- The Servicemembers Civil Relief Act (SCRA) is contained in Title 50 of the United States Code (50 U.S.C. App Section 501 et seq.). Rules regarding default judgments and stays of proceedings are found at sections 521 and 522.

- For more information on filing for divorce when one spouse is in the military, or is simply residing

124

out of the state or out of the country, see the Weinberger Law Group website: http://bit.ly/military-divorces.

- For a summary of information specific to military families, see the "Guide to Military Divorce" on the Weinberger Law Group website: http://bit.ly/military-guide.

- For an overview of post-judgment issues in New Jersey divorce, see the Weinberger Law Group website: http://bit.ly/post-divorce.

For More Information

At Weinberger Law Group all of our attorneys are engaged full time in the practice of family law. We understand that the stakes are high in your divorce and it is our mission to safeguard your children, protect your assets and secure your future. Our exclusive focus on divorce and family law enables us to create solutions that others may miss. Solutions that are caring, compassionate and right for your situation.

You can find out more about our dedicated family law attorneys on our website, which is located at www.WeinbergerLawGroup.com. Weinberger Law Group offers an initial consultation with an experienced New Jersey Family Law Attorney at no cost.

Weinberger Law Group has offices located throughout New Jersey.

Weinberger Law Group Headquarter Offices:
119 Cherry Hill Road, Suite 120
Parsippany, NJ 07054
Morris County

Tel: (888) 888-0919

Other Book Titles:
Weinberger Law Group Library Series
Of Family Law Guides

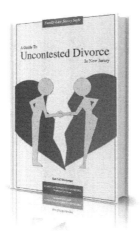

Uncontested Divorce

Child Support

Child Custody

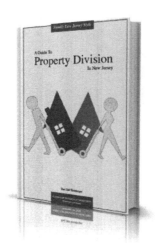

Property Division

Alimony

Ebook and print versions of the Weinberger Law Group Library series can be ordered via Amazon or by visiting www.WeinbergerLawGroup.com.

Made in the USA
Middletown, DE
19 November 2015